CINDY SOLONEC

Debesa

The Story of
Frank and Katie Rodriguez

Dear Monusen,
We hope this story transports
you to WA for at least a short
time this year.
We love & miss you
Ash & Dave xxx

Magabala
Books

This is a Magabala Book

LEADING PUBLISHER OF ABORIGINAL AND
TORRES STRAIT ISLANDER STORYTELLERS.

CHANGING THE WORLD, ONE STORY AT A TIME.

First published 2021

Magabala Books Aboriginal Corporation, Broome, Western Australia

Website: www.magabala.com Email: sales@magabala.com

Magabala Books receives financial assistance from the Commonwealth
Government through the Australia Council, its arts advisory body. The State of
Western Australia has made an investment in this project through the Department
of Local Government, Sport and Cultural Industries. Magabala Books would like
to acknowledge the generous support of the Shire of Broome, Western Australia.

Cover designed by Jo Hunt
Typeset by Post Pre-press Group
Printed and bound by Griffin Press South Australia

ISBN 978 1 925936 00 1

A catalogue record for this
book is available from the
National Library of Australia

NATIONAL
LIBRARY
OF AUSTRALIA

Department of
Local Government, Sport
and Cultural Industries
GOVERNMENT OF
WESTERN AUSTRALIA

lotterywest
supported

Australian Government

Australia
Council
for the Arts

Shire of
Broome
people · place · prosperity

For Pepita, Frank and Phillip

I acknowledge the traditional owners of this land and
I respect the laws and customs by forewarning that deceased
people's names are mentioned and images depicted. I ask that
individuals exercise caution when reading this book.

Contents

Foreword

My siblings, Pepita, Cindy and Phillip, and I were privileged to have lived and grown up on Debesa, a sheep station, with our parents who pioneered and made this special, isolated piece of land in the West Kimberley a place that we could all call home.

Our parents were very hard working and not wealthy people but were determined to pursue an opportunity of owning and developing their dream. Their cultural and spiritual backgrounds helped to create a future for all of us and with their combined Spanish, Aboriginal, English and Indian heritages, it has shaped our family history.

This book written by Cindy explores the unique and fascinating history of their journey that was taken largely from Dad's diaries dating back to the 1940s and until Mum passed away in 1994. He wrote first in Castilian and then later in English. She worked very hard with Dad to translate his diaries. Cindy was also privileged to have had many verbal stories relating to Mum and input by all of us and from Mum's siblings about her parents and Aboriginal heritage growing up in the Kimberley, including Beagle Bay and Drysdale River missions, Liveringa Station, in Derby and on Debesa. Cindy has been able to write about our parents and family history in this unique and special story and we are all grateful for her time and dedication.

Frank Rodriguez, Jnr

Preface

Out of sight and sitting quietly in my father's office, I rummaged through his papers, my school reports and his diaries. Dad had begun jotting down snippets from his life in 1944 after moving to the Kimberley. The diaries intrigued me as they did my siblings, Pepita, Frank and Phillip. As kids, we entertained illusions of some discerning writer delving into his memoirs to reveal a Spaniard's romanticised story. Surely, his and our mother's encounter was their destiny – a love story to be told.

Growing up on Debesa Station 100 kilometres east of Derby in the West Kimberley, we were the children of working-class people who had had little formal education, and none of us had any idea of what was involved in writing a book – or who to even approach. Like my siblings I was rather smug that my Dad, Frank Rodriguez, who had come to Australia to be a Benedictine monk, had met and married my mum,

Katie Fraser, instead. She also had been a novitiate in an abbey, in fact, in a convent for 'black' women at Beagle Bay Mission, 130 kilometres north of Broome. It's no surprise then that us kids had a firm grounding in Catholicism.

I often wondered why Dad even kept a diary. Was it a companion in whom he could confide in undisturbed solitude, far from his childhood home in Galicia in the northwest of Spain? Or perhaps it helped him sharpen his English skills. Some diarists, it is said, cannot even explain why they keep writing. It's like an addiction. My dad's diaries are far from intimate portrayals of his emotions and conundrums. On the contrary, the entries of two or three sentences can be quite bland. His imperfect English generally depicts the weather, his working day and his God. Dad, an autodidact, had a Brownie box camera and he loved capturing family photos that inadvertently complemented his diaries.

By the late 1990s, thirty years after my parents had left Debesa, no-one had emerged showing interest in the diaries, so I found a way to make use of his legacy – or so I thought. I had decided to do a master's research degree exploring coexistence on Nigena (Nyikina) country. I had worked briefly at the National Native Title Tribunal where, under the 'Act', Aboriginal land claimants had to demonstrate their coexistence with gudia (non-Aboriginal) people. Despite having inhabited these lands for thousands of years, it was our mob who had to prove their continued presence in their own countries, demonstrating their existence to gudia, who had only been here for five minutes. It meant that my countrimin (Aboriginal people) had to research and articulate coexistence as determined by white people.

Surely then, I convinced myself, my father's diaries would be a treasure trove of examples about Aboriginal people's way of life on the stations. After all, he had lived and worked in the region for many, many years. Moreover, he knew a lot of our mob. Through my master's, I believed I could convincingly demonstrate Aboriginal coexistence with other 'interested parties'. So I asked him if I could use his diaries and he was happy to bequeath them to me: 'I'd thought about throwing them out, no-one ...' he sighed, 'was interested in them.' Excited about this undertaking, I arranged for Dad to come to Perth and translate the first six years of his entries that were all written in Spanish.

Cindy and Frank – Yokine, 2003
© *Kylie Gibson, photographer*

Time had taken its toll on the diaries. They were now yellow and brittle and not always readable. As we thumbed delicately through the pages, like confetti, tiny bits of paper fell onto the desk. He peered closely at the entry for 2 February 1948 and mused, 'Can't ... quite ... read ... what I've written here – but the cockroaches will know what it says.'

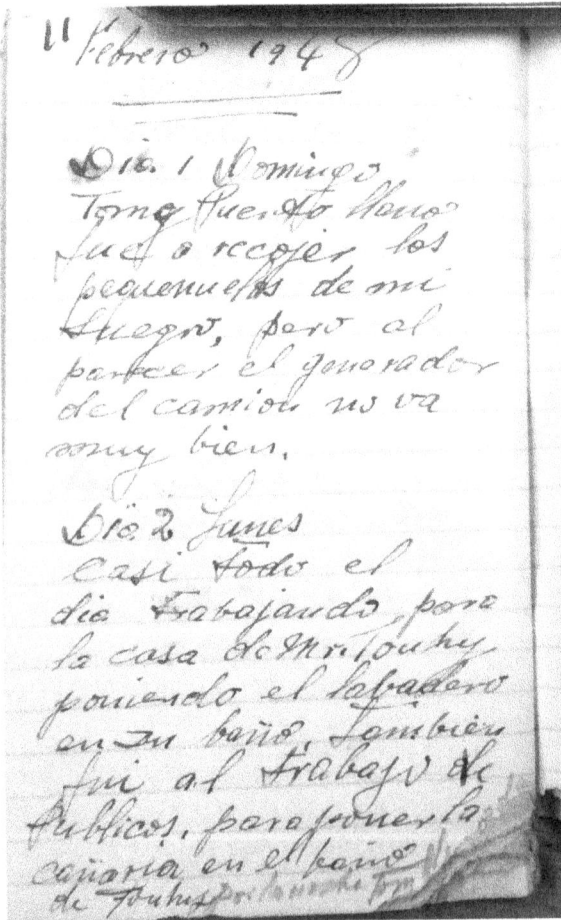

2 February 1948, Frank Rodriguez, diarist

We sat for two weeks at my home in Yokine, a Perth suburb, enjoying our time together and reliving his early days in the Kimberley. Sometimes I probed him about the more cryptic entries, like on Wednesday, 3 September 1947: 'All day working for Watt. Tonight we had several visits from half a moon.' I mischievously asked him whether this was about his and Mum's moonlight shenanigans. He told me to mind my own business. Dad had a great sense of humour, often at his own expense. Like the time he learned to ride a horse, on a mule. The mule, he reckoned, knew he was a 'new chum' and threw him, to the chortles of the Aboriginal stockmen.

Why I ever thought my father would write specifically about Aboriginal peoples, or any ethnic group, is beyond me. He didn't even write about how gudia people lived. His diaries lacked the copious descriptions of the daily reality for Nigena people that I had hoped they would. He had just penned his day-to-day endeavours. Consequently, I hardly used his memoirs for the master's thesis that I completed in 2003.

Still wanting to contribute to recording how my folks had lived, I embarked on a PhD in 2010 – an extension of my master's thesis. I was keen to leave a documented account for posterity about the way marginalised peoples lived in the Mardoowarra (Fitzroy River) region during the middle of the twentieth century. A social history as experienced by my families. I wanted to leave an account of ordinary people's everyday lives that would not otherwise be recorded. An account based on my parents' joint biography.

The diaries became an invaluable source as the chronological framework for my five-year PhD project. At last, they were receiving the attention I had convinced myself they deserved. Perhaps, too, my childhood fantasy of a love story would emerge. I would come to realise this was a 'forbidden' love story under white people's condescending attitudes to relationships between Aboriginal people and gudia.

Delving into Dad's diaries, I was excited to find the entries were sparsely dotted with gems about our extended families. I yearned for more. If only my mother had left a written account of her day-to-day life, this story would have had an even richer and broader perspective. Fortunately for me though, Aboriginal peoples still uphold past events through oral histories. For my master's I had invited them to tell me what they knew about life in the region during my folks' time. They had obliged willingly. I was excited to find that their stories were not that hard to cross-reference with the literature. Their memory vaults with stories that have been handed down served them well, confirming the reliability of Indigenous intelligence. As well as Dad's diaries, this family history features quotes by family members from interviews and yarns I've had with them over the years.

I was keen now to know more about my Australian great-grandparents. I knew that, to know who my mother was, I had to give them a voice. So as I listened to my family's narratives, my ancestors began to emerge in an almost life-like way. I was beginning to 'know' Granny's parents even though they had died some twenty years before I was born. Grampa's parents, too, started to make their presence felt. Along with their narratives and by peeking into mission, pastoral and town archives, the past began speaking to the now and I brought them into the present. No longer were they banished and forgotten.

I don't claim to know what my parents' feelings were. No-one can ever know the profound and philosophical thoughts of an individual, no matter how close to someone you are. One can only speculate. But what I do know is that it was my parents' shared faith, their cultural values and the children of their union that formed the strength of their relationship.

This is their story.

Acknowledgements

I am grateful to my parents, Katie and Frank Rodriguez, for their contribution to our family history. I had interviewed Mum about her school days shortly before she passed in 1994; and Dad, as a young non-English speaking foreigner to the Kimberley in 1944, started a diary that became the chronological framework for this story. I am grateful for the unconditional support from Dieter and our daughters, Kylie and Tammy, and my siblings Pepita Pregelj and Frank Rodriguez, who made comment and corrections. My younger brother Phillip's memories, I was delighted to find, are similar to my own. I am indebted to my aunties Eddie and Leena Fraser, who kept me informed of extended family history and Nigena culture.

This book would not have been possible without the generosity of people who gave me their stories and/or access to relevant documents over several years: Aggie Puertollano, Gertie AhMat, Jim Fraser, Frances Ward, Kerry McCarthy, Pat Bergmann,

Cyril Puertollano, Shirley Rickerby, Phillipa Cook, Dickie and Patsy Yambo, Tony Ozies, June and Henry Gooch, Audrey Bullough, Keven Rose, Marie Megaw, Pat Begley, Patsy Millet, Phil Bianchi, Fr David Barry, Fr Bernard Rooney and Fr Anscar McPhee. Relatives in Spain, Jackie Vazquez and Javier Gonzalez, and from Sydney, Manuel Gonzalez, clarified my email queries. Others include librarians, archivists and moral supporters. Other worthy contributors include Anne Poelina, Christine Bergmann, Damien Parriman, Helen Bergmann, Wayne Bergmann and Marcia Finger, the owner of Debesa Station. On occasions with Dad and with my siblings Pepita or Phillip, I have visited Debesa where Marcia kindly encouraged us to drive through familiar country.

To my theses supervisors Peggy Brock (MA), Charlie Fox, Andrea Gaynor and the wonderful Shino Konishi (PhD), thank you. And, finally, Rae Luckie, who mentored me in the early stages of writing, and later, publishing editors Margaret Whiskin and Kelly Somers.

My gratitude is extended to one and all.

The spelling of Aboriginal words

Linguists and anthropologists have developed the spelling of Aboriginal words over time from the way in which they hear a word. Today, in conjunction with Aboriginal speakers, some Australian languages have official orthographies, yet a variety of spellings remain. In this book, as the author, I choose to spell my grandparents' and our Aboriginal country's names phonetically as Jira (Sara), Yoolya (Eulla) and Nigena (Nyikina) respectively.

When words other than English first appear in this book, I explain them just the once, in brackets, straight after the word or text. For example, Mardoowarra (Fitzroy River, *Nigena*), sobrino (nephew, *Spanish*). Today, many Aboriginal words have spread beyond their country of origin and are used broadly across regions.

Nigena

Nigena country is where my family's Aboriginal heritage originates. Both my maternal grandparents, Yoolya and Jira, were born on Nigena country. The Kimberley is where four of their eight children lived and it is where many of their descendants continue to live today. Moreover, my parents lived all their married life on Nigena country. It is where they met, married and where their four children were born. All their ten grandchildren were born in the Kimberley.

In respect to my ancestors, I opt to use the spelling 'Nigena', which best reflects the way we have always pronounced our Aboriginality. Over the years, anthropologists and linguists have spelt the term phonetically as 'Nigena', 'Njigina', 'Nyigina' and 'Njigana'. Today, the official orthographical spelling is 'Nyikina'.

Introduction

From the time Western colonisers forced their way on to Aboriginal lands, they had deemed the humans already here a nuisance. The colonisers had become fixated on wiping my ancestors out. They were hell-bent on destroying Australia's Indigenous cultures and erasing black peoples from the nation's psyche. But it is through their official files, documents and journals that our post-contact histories survive. The colonisers left the perfect paper trail.

They were ignorant of the fact that people had lived here for thousands of years. Ignorant of sophisticated Indigenous ways of living that were complete with customs, belief systems, kinship patterns, cultural interactions and trading routes. But not ignorant of a pre-colonial economy, it seems. Our Aboriginal ancestors had worked the Australian landscape in various ways. Their resourcefulness is extolled in those paper trails – the journals of early explorers. Seeds were harvested and stored, fish traps and river dams built and permanent shelters erected that the early colonists noticed, but dismissed, preferring instead to promote Australia's Indigenous peoples as 'hunter-gatherers' roaming the landscape in search of food. A convenient untruth.

To westerners the Kimberley was rugged and inhospitable in climate and terrain. This perspective was, for a brief moment, overturned by the explorer Alexander Forrest in the late 1870s. The younger brother of Western Australia's first premier, John Forrest, he enthusiastically gave a robust assessment of the region as being ideal for pastoralism. A land grab followed. Without any consultation with the Aboriginal owners, gudia pastoralists were offered leases, some as large as one million acres. Alexander Forrest likened the region to the gold-bearing country around Pine Creek in the Northern Territory, leading to the first, and only, short-lived gold rush in the Kimberley from 1886 to 1889.

By the late 1890s the pastoral industry had expanded. In the northeast Kimberley, colonialists from the eastern colonies, Francis Connor, Denis Doherty and Michael and Patrick Durack, joined together to form a pastoral company. In the west Kimberley, influential Perth-based men like Alexander Forrest and Isadore Emanuel snapped up leases. Together these inter-lopers' properties eventually morphed into the beef-producing empires of Western Australia.

In the early years of the pastoral industry, sheep stations emerged along the lower Mardoowarra valley on the homelands of Nigena people. This country was among the last Indigenous homelands in Western Australia to be appropriated for pasto-ralism. The land grabbers included the Cornish brothers Hamlet and Anthony, who took up a run between Beagle Bay and the

Mardoowarra and called it Yeeda Station, 25 kilometres from Derby. Their initial descriptions of the people living there were flattering: 'We noticed they were a fine race of men, athletic, tall and muscular, no covering whatever, with the exception of a woven band, about an inch wide, round their waists. A few emu feathers, and a small bone through their nose, which indicated full dress.'

It didn't take long before the intruders turned on the locals. The pastoralists claimed that our people were a 'problem'. Their presence, they protested, hindered their pastoral efforts. Not only did their stock have to compete with Aboriginal people for pasture, Aboriginals found the sheep a tasty and easy to capture meat source. It was stealing, the pastoralists lamented, and took the law into their own hands. Distant from authorities in faraway Perth and often fearing for their lives, they took to killing Aboriginal people across the Kimberley as a method of control. 'Bush justice', they called it.

Some of the station owners moved into colonial politics, as did Connor and Forrest, who became powerful figures. Entrenched in the Western Australian Legislative Council, they ruthlessly pursued their pastoral interests, passing legislation to regulate Aboriginal employment in their favour. Moreover, with ever-increasing severity, they used the offence of 'sheep stealing' as a cover to imprison Aboriginal people on whose country their stations had been marked out.

Police were initially introduced to the Kimberley in the 1880s and those who tried to protect the Aboriginals were removed and replaced with police who sided with the pastoralists. They dealt with 'offenders' in cruel and harsh ways. Slaughtering them or shackling people together with neck chains and forcing them to walk hundreds of miles to jails, to be put on ships that took them to far-off places, never to return. Most were men, though women and teenagers were also known to have been captured. Still, our people fought back. The central Kimberley resistance fighter Jandamarra defied the newcomers' demands that he be implicated in massacres of his own Bunuba people, and he was one of many who made life difficult for the invaders.

In Nigena country, from the time the Cornish brothers arrived, our people resisted them. They fought back. A war between the locals and the westerners continued until my countrimin succumbed to the 'conquest of the gun' and worked on their station. Under colonial rule they became a vital asset in the development of the Kimberley pastoral industry. Without black labour, those properties would have struggled and not even survived.

Further south, under the direction of Western Australian government surveyor Alfred Canning, the Canning Stock Route opened in the early 1900s. A conduit to muster East Kimberley stock to southern markets. It ran from Billiluna Station south of Halls Creek to the township of Wiluna in the goldfields, from where stock was loaded onto trains for Geraldton, Midland and Fremantle. Stock routes deliberately ran close to desert people's precious soaks, which were made into wells, rendering their long-established water sources inaccessible.

The route bridged many Aboriginal countries. Cruel tactics were used to force desert people to reveal their water sources. Shackled together at night and given salt, they became thirsty and had little choice but to lead Canning's men to the water. Furthermore, gudia men pursued their women and stole

Aboriginal property. Our people fought back. They vandalised at least half the wells by removing the buckets and setting timber casings alight, succeeding in stopping the interlopers for several years. The route recommenced in the 1930s.

On our Nigena homelands, gudia men engaged in sexual interactions with Aboriginal women, either by consent or rape. Mixed-descent children began appearing on the Kimberley landscape where few gudia men accepted responsibility for them. The 1886 *Aborigines Protection Act* didn't protect these children. That piece of legislation was concerned with the employment of Aboriginal people. Teenagers from the age of fourteen could be employed as cheap labour, while kids as young as six were known to have been working for the pastoralists. Aboriginal workers were not entitled to any cash pay. Just flour, sugar and tea.

Concern about the abuse mounted and pressure brought on by worried humanitarians triggered a survey into the administration of Aboriginal peoples. Of particular interest was the interaction between Aboriginal and non-Aboriginal. Both the state government and missionaries were concerned that the exploitation and mistreatment of Aboriginal women was resulting in growing numbers of 'half-caste' children. So they engaged in passionate discussions about who our mob should and should not have relationships with.

A dislike for Asian people was evident, therefore it was relationships between Asian men and Aboriginal women that worried the 'powers that be' the most. Consequently, their debates manoeuvred around the ideology that everyone must live like white people. Speak their language. Adapt to their ways. And marry lighter skinned people until Australia was rid of dark-skinned people. Such deliberations continued from the 1930s to the 1970s and beyond. An attempt to control cohabitation between races had, in part, been the catalyst for the *Aborigines Act 1905* (WA). The new rules, under the guise of protectionism, allowed for tighter controls over our people well into the twentieth century. The 1905 Act, as it became known, gave government officials the legal right to remove 'mixed-descent' children from their families.

A new position came with the act – the Chief Protector of Aborigines. This position covered the whole of Western Australia. To help him do his job, the Chief Protector could appoint proxy protectors, who were often policemen. So began a long and uneasy relationship between Aboriginal peoples and the police. From that time on, my grandparents came under the control of a government authority who plotted with missionaries to take children from their families. Not surprisingly, little attention was ever given to 'full-descent' people. They were expected to just die out.

In 1907 Charles Frederick Gale became the Chief Protector in Western Australia. On being told there were numerous 'half-caste' children in the Kimberley, he reacted by claiming that they would be better off on missions. He even assumed that 'mixed-descent' kids were more intelligent than 'black' kids. He had no qualms about taking them from their mothers. His travelling inspector for Aborigines, James Isdell, in the late 1890s claimed, 'I would not hesitate for one moment to separate any half-caste from its Aboriginal mother, no matter how frantic her momentary grief might be at the time. They soon forget their offspring.'

Consequently, my mixed-descent grandparents were legally taken from their black mothers. Snatched by police off Nigena country, both were very young when they were displaced to Kimberley Catholic missions in 1909. Catholicism would profoundly impact their descendants, denying us the inherent right to embrace our own Nigena culture and language.

My Granny's bush name was Jira, which in all likelihood sounded like Sara, because that is the name that first appeared in reference to her in a report from Beagle Bay to the Chief Protector. But there is no 'c' nor 's' in Aboriginal languages. Jira was sent to the Pallottine mission at Beagle Bay on Nyul Nyul lands north of Broome and given the western name 'Phillipena'.

Grampa, too, had his bush name, 'Yoolya', meddled with. His name is spelled as 'Eulla' in most of the official documents – the way in which Europeans heard it. Yoolya was taken to the Benedictine mission at Drysdale River on the northernmost tip of Western Australia and given the name 'Fulgentius' after the incumbent bishop, Fulgentius Torres.

Many years later, when asked by her daughter Edna how she came to be at Beagle Bay, Granny began to cry, '... they locked us in Derby jail house'.

CHAPTER 1

Removed

*They listened to their distraught mothers
call them from near the cell*

Jimmy Casim was my maternal great-grandfather. A teenager when he sailed into Fremantle from India in the 1880s, he was a deckhand on an Indian cargo vessel with his uncle as the bosun. He had come at a time when ships from the subcontinent made several trips a year, back and forth from Karachi. They brought teams of Afghan cameleers and their camels to Australia for the opening up of the inland and it was on one of those trips that Jimmy became ill. With his uncle's prompting, he jumped ship to get help. The young seafarer stayed in Western Australia and, like others from his part of the world, he merged into a life of indentured labour.

Nygumi (grandfather), as his grandchildren called him, ventured north into Ngarluma country in the Pilbara to the coastal town of Cossack. There, tin shacks and sturdy stone buildings were burgeoning in hilly outcrops that fronted a seemingly tranquil Indian Ocean. In the bustling town he blended well among the 989 Malays and 493 Aboriginals, many who worked the vessels that searched for pearl shell off the coast. With a large Asian population, Cossack had its own Chinatown and Nygumi settled into working on the dry docks.

By 1886 the Pilbara pearling industry was flagging. As fewer boats operated from Cossack, a parliamentary select committee recommended its closure as a pearling hub and the industry moved to Broome. Nygumi followed. He had an uncle there who employed him as a pearl diver. In Broome he was able to embrace his Muslim faith in the company of Muslim Malays and impassioned Indonesians.

But it was Aboriginal communities that he was drawn to. Nygumi found work as a camp cook at Yeeda Station, a 700,000-acre lease 180 kilometres north of Broome on the Mardoowarra in Nigena country. It is where he met the beautiful Muninga, a Nigena woman. They had a daughter in 1900 and called her Jira – she was my Granny. Born on the banks of the Mardoowarra, her birth date, 1 January, is one that was given to Aboriginals in the early days of colonisation. Either that or 1 July.

My families took for granted how the majestic Mardoowarra with its many tributaries weaved its way through Nigena country and beyond. They knew that Woonyoomboo, a Nigena creation ancestor, was the first to travel along the Nigena section of the river before he became a rufous night heron. He can still be heard, singing in the trees. Together, my great-grandparents watched and listened and Nygumi came to appreciate my great-grandmother's culture. Local creation stories hold our Nigena history and they explain our people's relationship to the river, to the land and to our liyan (deep feelings). Given his own Muslim beliefs, Nygumi had respect for Muninga's customs. He came to revere her people's inherited connection to the Mardoowarra and their Nigena homelands which had never been lost to them.

My great-grandmother lived happily enough with their extended family, which included Numingil, Muninga's sister, and her daughter, Gypsy, who was just a little younger than my Granny. Living in the camp too was Eddy Yedewarra, one of Muninga's Nigena husbands. During the day while the men mustered stock and tended to station jobs, the children fished with their mothers, 'steering clear of crocodiles', Granny laughed years later. Most evenings everyone joined in ceremonies, dancing and singing. The families sometimes lived in the bush, especially during Lore time, to the west and to the north of the Yeeda homestead – a way of life that was gradually being denied them as pastoralists moved sheep and cattle onto Nigena lands. The women sometimes walked the 20-kilometre track to Derby to find work, the kids playing along the way, hiding in the bush, collecting bush food, chattering and laughing.

At Mayalls Well (Myalls Bore), a few kilometres south of the town, they rested. Nearby was a large potbelly boab tree that had been used to lock up Aboriginal prisoners in the late 1800s. Oral histories reveal that it was used as a jail cell right up into the twentieth century. It mystified Muninga and Numingil that their countrimin had been imprisoned inside or chained to the outside of that tree.

The prisoners had arrived there after walking for hundreds of kilometres from the east and from the north, harnessed together with chains. Suffering weight loss and with deep wounds from chains around their necks, shoulders and wrists, the men had been forced to walk for days along inland routes. Constable Pilger at Fitzroy Crossing, 160 kilometres to the east, boasted about the cat-o'-nine-tails he used to flog blackfullas. Escorted to Derby by mounted, armed police to be sentenced for crimes that no-one understood – except for gudia – they were deported south to jails at Irremugadu (Roebourne) and Wadjemup (Rottnest Island). They perished off-country.

It was mid-1909 when Muninga and Numingil, while working for Quan Sing, a Chinese shop owner, had their children stolen from them. As they raked and cleaned up the yard and the children played outside, two policemen came by on horse and cart, on the prowl for 'half-caste' kids. With them were two Aboriginal offsiders. Under the rules of the *Aborigines Act 1905* it was legal for the police to just snatch kids who weren't of 'full descent' from their parents. The law had come about because colonists and humanitarians were of the mindset that the half-black, half-white kids would be better off away from their black mothers and brought up on missions. Furthermore, they claimed that the children would be better protected from exploitation by pastoralists.

The police, helped by their offsider who spoke in Nigena, lured the little girls to the cart with lollies. Realising what was going on, their friend Albert ran away and hid as they excitedly hopped up onto the cart. 'Come on Albert', they called after him, 'we going ride.' Albert watched from behind the shop and when all was clear, he ran to tell Muninga and Numingil. Their hearts sank. They knew. Word had reached them too late to protect their children.

The girls were taken to the Derby lockup and given a crusty old blanket to lay on the grimy concrete floor of a caged cell.

Edna Fraser, Old Derby Gaol, 2015.
Each cell 7.5 m x 5 m © Kylie Gibson, photographer

Together they huddled next to large iron loops that were fixed into the floor, where adult prisoners had been shackled and fed flour and water. Chained in gangs, our countrimin had been forced into hard labour to develop the town and were returned to the cells at night. In fact, the site was used as a prison up until the 1970s.

Frightened in the dark, Gypsy, who was still being breast-fed cried, 'Mumma nanya (breast),' while a scared Jira tried to keep her quiet, whispering, 'Shhh, leinju (policeman) coming.' Faces swollen and sticky with tears and dust, they clung to each other as they listened to their distraught mothers call them from near the cell. The police ignored the commotion.

Early the next morning they were boarded onto a tram and taken to the jetty. As the tram trundled slowly across the 2-kilometre stretch of barren marsh between the town and the jetty, they struggled to get away but a policeman held them so tightly their little arms hurt. Their mothers ran alongside shouting to them. Realising the hopelessness of the situation, Muninga fell to the ground and picked up a rock. She smashed her head repeatedly until blood streamed down her face, down her arms and dripped from her fingers to the ground, blending into the red dirt. It was her way of grieving. At the jetty the children were put in the care of an Aboriginal woman from Queensland for the long boat journey to Beagle Bay Mission, southeast of Derby on the Dampier Peninsula.

In the early 1900s the Adelaide Steamship Company operated a fleet of twenty-seven stock and passenger carriers between Fremantle, the eastern states and the northwest. There were steam tugs, steam lighters and coal hulks. The ships that sailed along the Western Australian coast, serviced by local agents, also carried human cargo. Aboriginal prisoners and children who had been taken from their families were placed together in the cattle carriers. After all, it was the Department of Aborigines and Fisheries in Perth that made decisions about our people.

On a clear night in July of 1909, the SS *Koombana* manoeuvred its way through numerous small islands in the Buccaneer Archipelago heading to Derby on high tide. A brand-new, state-of-the-art passenger and cargo ship, it had only arrived at Fremantle from England in early 1909 to service the northwest ports. Now it was on its fifth trip to Derby in the same year.

Named after one of several properties owned by the Forrests, a pioneering family near Bunbury in the south, 'koombana' means calm and peaceful in Noongar, the Aboriginal language from the southwest. The SS *Koombana* berthed at the Derby jetty where passengers were greeted enthusiastically by the townspeople, who in turn were invited aboard. The visitors wallowed in the ship's luxurious decor, its elegant dining rooms and cabins, socialising until it was time for the ship to leave on its return voyage to Fremantle. Were the Derby folk even aware of the two terrified little girls in the lower decks next to countrimin in chains and a menagerie of plumped-up cattle, chickens and dogs to boot?

Numingil and Yedewarra followed the children while Muninga, too traumatised to go anywhere, agreed to stay in Derby. The two set out on the 300-kilometre trek from Derby to Beagle Bay. Walking through Yeeda Station on country they knew well, camping at Mount Jowlaenga and crossing the Fraser River, they were not short of sustenance – feasting on introduced stock. In Derby, Muninga pined for her daughter, who was never off her mind, and wondered when she might see her again. She waited in Derby, just in case Jira came back.

The journey by ship to Broome and then on the mission supply lugger to Beagle Bay terrified the bewildered little cousin-sisters. They had no idea where they were going or why they had been taken away from their mothers. At the mission they joined forty-four girls and forty boys from across the Kimberley. Called orphans, they were promptly baptised and given Christian names. Jira became 'Phillipena' and Gypsy became 'Francesca'.

Dormitory children, 1910, Beagle Bay Mission
© *Pallottine Archives*

Beagle Bay Mission was established in 1890 by the French Trappist monks. By 1901 they couldn't cope financially and abandoned their aspirations. The German Pallottines stepped in and in 1907 the Sisters of St John of God came to run the school and the girls' dormitory.

In his 'Return of Children' report to the Protector of Aborigines for the quarter ending September 1909, the German priest Fr Joseph Bischofs listed another twenty-five children at Beagle Bay. Their details included a number, name, ethnicity, sex, age and date of admission. Granny was listed as '2. Phil. Sara Tierer. H.C. Girl. 6. July 1908'.

It was not unusual for records to have dates inconsistent with events; the *Koombana* actually visited Derby for the first time six months after July 1908. In the book *This is Your Place*, a collection of stories from Beagle Bay inmates edited by Fr Francis Huegel and Sr Brigida Nailon, Granny names the *Koombana* as the ship that she and Gypsy travelled on to Broome. People's names too were often spelt several different ways. It left me wondering what the word 'tierer' might mean in this context, given that in German 'tiere' means 'animals'. Was Bischofs declaring that my 'half-caste' grandmother was 'mongrel' since her father was not European but Indian?

The children's new home was an evolving mission with just a few buildings, including a school and a church that stood side by side. Made from mud bricks and local timbers with thatched roofs, the huts were susceptible to white ants. Nestled on the outskirts of the mission, the bush people lived in rudimentary humpies shaped from sticks, leaves and tin sheets, with old blankets for comfort. It is where Numingil and Yedewarra camped. From time to time, they travelled the route across Yeeda to Derby to see Muninga. At Beagle Bay they saw the children often. Together they talked to them over the fence, making sure they knew who they were and where they had come from. Neither of my grannies ever forgot their homelands.

Now they were forced to live on Nyul Nyul country. The local people, despite the intrusion of Christianity, continued their Lore commitments, in particular, customary law like malulu – initiation rites for male youth. Nyul Nyul men stood firm in what they knew was the right thing to do, frustrating the Catholic priests' attempts to interfere and annihilate their customs.

Sometime later, when the mission's church and the school were destroyed in a cyclone, a new church began to emerge. Almost everyone on the mission helped to build a much sturdier building, even the two little girls from Yeeda. The children gathered sizeable quantities of shell from the nearby beach – trochus and huge clams – while splashing and playing in the water as the men loaded the shells onto bullock-drawn carts. Piled high, each batch was delivered to the building site, burned and processed for mortar. Bricks were shaped by hand from a combination of local muds, baked in a kiln, then cemented together with the mortar. The outer walls were whitewashed with a substance made from pounded cooked shells.

My two grannies were maturing into well-grounded young women. Despite an imposed Western lifestyle, they both kept close to Numingil and Yedewarra. Muninga, meantime, lived in the hope that the girls were safe. Knowing that Numingil was with them did give her some peace of mind, but she never knew exactly where they were. From talking with others, she knew the girls were with people in white clothes. Like a crumbled old photograph she held this news close to her heart. It was all she had.

———

The Spanish Benedictine monks at New Norcia, 125 kilometres north of Perth, made moves in the early 1900s to start a mission in the northernmost reaches of the state. There was a degree of urgency because they had competition. A few years earlier the Anglicans had begun setting up Forrest River Mission, 50 kilometres west of Wyndham in the East Kimberley, though after one year they abandoned it because of a series of attacks by the local people. Some Anglicans considered that mob to be 'savage aboriginals, who hurled several spears at the missionaries', so they left and headed to central Australia, where the Lutherans had already taken hold. But now, after recovering from their injuries in Perth, a few were heading back to continue their missionary endeavours. To offset their plans the Benedictines moved quickly because they, too, wanted to save the 'poor neglected aborigines' from being harassed and slaughtered by pastoralists in far northern Western Australia.

With no time to lose, the Abbot of New Norcia, Fulgentius Torres, set about getting permission from the West Australian government to establish a mission. He sailed on the SS *Bullara* on 27 April 1906, heading for Broome. There, he sourced help to reach his destination in the Joseph Bonaparte Gulf 3,500 kilometres from Perth and 800 kilometres north of Broome by sea, at a time when the area was inaccessible by road. He hired a small 14-ton schooner, the *San Salvador*, from Father Emo, a Trappist priest in Broome, and engaged the priest's services along with a Captain Johnson and four Manila men. Undeterred by treacherous waters over uncharted reefs, the Abbot and his troupe set sail for the gulf region.

Along the way they explored several inlets until they reached an area with good soil and water. The area is called Pago by the local Kwini and Kulari people. It is where the Benedictines believed they were most needed. Fr Emo himself had already identified Pago some years earlier as a suitable place for a second mission, but his ambitions were never realised because he was under pressure from the Pallottines to progress refuges in Broome and at Beagle Bay. Now it was the Benedictines who would establish their mission on the Drysdale River at Pago.

Around this area early explorers had reported seeing many Aboriginal men running frenziedly along the beach towards them waving spears. They were described as tall men, like giants. Similarly, when whitefullas started intruding on our country in the 1880s in the Beagle Bay and Yeeda Station region, Hamlet Cornish claimed to have seen numerous 'natives' who did not like his party coming onto their country and meant war against them. He described our men as being 'athletic, tall and muscular'. For fear of being 'swarmed' by the local people, Cornish's party warded them off by firing shots over their heads, scattering countrimin through the thickly timbered bush. The difference between the pastoralists and the missionaries is that the latter came armed with prayer to subdue the Aboriginals, while Cornish's men were armed with revolvers and rifles and plenty of ammunition. Indeed, Australia had introduced a form of gun control early in the colonisation era. On the east coast those considered as 'worthless characters' like convicts and trigger-happy 'settlers' had to register their firearms. Moreover, Arthur Phillip went on to advise the British government that Aboriginals in the area 'are sensible of the great superiority of our arms'. He was worried they might retaliate forcefully to the invasion if they had access to firearms.

Torres's evidence was tangible. He saw fires in the area – smoke during the day – and numerous people and dogs. All along the coast, campfires confirmed the presence of Aboriginals. Mistreatment by pastoralists had left those in the northern reaches sceptical of interlopers, so they forced the monks to remain incognito for the first two years as they warded them off and protected their country. Not put off, the Benedictines named their emerging sanctuary Drysdale River Mission.

Drysdale River Mission, The W.A. Record, 27 December 1919

Meanwhile, southeast of Yeeda Station, another large pastoral lease had claimed more of the Mardoowarra and its floodplains. Liveringa, a one-million-acre sheep station 120 kilometres from Derby, had been taken up by the Kimberley Pastoral Company (KPC). It comprised a consortium of wealthy businessmen from down south, including Premier John Forrest. Liveringa was a robust, bustling station with a lot of potential, according to the KPC, and it already had one million sheep. Rivers, billabongs and bores with plenty of water complemented the emerging buildings, stables and fences. The lessees even claimed that Liveringa was 'full of adventure and excitement heightened by the hostility of the natives'. Aboriginals laid claim to sheep meat that the pastoralists declared was theft.

On stations along the Mardoowarra, land was fundamental to Nigena existence. They knew every part of that country intimately. Their neighbours and the broader Australian first people's concept of 'country', their religious attachment, their awareness of food sources, was inherent to their way of life. They knew the call, cry and track of every living creature. Everything that breathed, every hill, every creek, crevice and outcrop and the night sky with its myriad of galaxies, they knew by name. The seasons dictated their movements and their care for country within pliable boundaries. No-one ever got lost.

Nigena station hands watched as their land was taken from them for pastoralism. They were distraught. Sacred places were given Western names and destroyed by hooved animals and by fences, windmills, tanks and water troughs. My extended family, like refugees in their own country, lived in bush camps near the homesteads after having surrendered to working for the bosses. To muddy the destruction of Aboriginal culture, lecherous, irresponsible gudia menfolk found our women appealing.

Liveringa is where my maternal grandfather Yoolya – who we called Grampa – was born on 1 July 1899, under a tree not far from the present-day Camballin homestead. His mother was

Wadadarl (Brumby), a Nigena woman, and his biological father was Percy Rose, a gudia stockman who worked for the KPC.

On his native welfare file, Grampa's mum is identified as Brumby FB. Brumby was her Western name and FB meant 'full blood'. She died when Grampa was a toddler and he was then looked after by her sister Stumpy – his other mum. Little is known about his mothers and it is unlikely that either ever left the bush life. And it's unlikely that either of my great-grandmothers ever learned Christianity. Grampa, on the other hand, was being influenced by Europeans while still learning Nigena customs. He was being skilled up in station work when Walter Fraser, a sheep overseer, became his legal guardian as a favour to Percy Rose, who had become the Liveringa manager in 1900.

Walter Fraser (far left) Noonkanbah, 1915.
State Library of Western Australia (b2862178_7)

Rose, an honorary protector of Aborigines and a justice of the peace, probably harboured a sense of responsibility for his biological son, so he gave Walter Fraser £500 to be Grampa's legal guardian. Rose would have been aware that under Section 34 of the 1905 Act, any gudia with a child under the age of fourteen who was in the care of missionaries or the government had to pay support. I hazard a guess that, given his distinguished status and given he knew full well that Grampa would be removed to a mission, Percy Rose subtly abided by the law.

Walter Fraser was a tall man with an impressive white handlebar moustache that complemented his thin, greying hair. He looked every bit the Scotsman that he was. Fraser had grown up on his father's crofter farm shepherding sheep and hoeing turnips before coming to Australia. It's uncertain how old he was when he arrived but he worked in the eastern states for a while as a coach driver for Cobb and Co.

It was his experience on some of the biggest sheep stations in the east that prepared him for work in the West Kimberley. Fraser could handle large numbers of sheep and he was used to the way in which sheep were sheared with clippers. He worked for several years on Liveringa, where he preferred to live at outstations rather than homesteads. He cut timber for fence posts and he built humpies with the help of Aboriginal stockmen, or, as Rose called my countrimin, 'natives' or 'niggers'. As his foster great grandchildren who he never knew, we would in time become familiar with the place names where Walter Fraser worked, mostly in the far reaches of the vast lease: Mount Wynne, Nooranoorah, Moolaman, Yuralla, Camballin and Willumbah.

Every couple of years Fraser travelled to Perth by ship to check on his properties down south, according to Harold Godbehear. In his book, *Kimberley was God's*, Godbehear says the old man was eventually ripped off by some women in Perth and he lost everything. Walter Fraser is believed to have died intestate down south, perhaps in the mid-1900s since he reappears in Grampa's native welfare file in 1940.

The station's bush people liked Walter Fraser. They looked after him and he looked out for them. His method of salting and carving a killer (sheep or bullock) for the camp mob is described in spirited fashion by Godbehear: 'With knife aloft he brought it down with a swish across the dampers and salt junk, bunged one upon the other and shot the portion along the oat bag spread before him, muttering a native name.' Fraser always had a Bible in his swag so he may well have been the first to plant ideas of Christianity in young Yoolya's mind.

Like my grandmother, Grampa was safe with his family living in the camp with Stumpy the day he was forcibly removed. His second-eldest daughter, Aggie Puertollano, explained in 2003 that Fraser didn't look after Grampa, his Aboriginal father did: 'Fulgentius for Fraser from Walter, but he never looked after Grampa, his Aboriginal father looked after him.' Two months earlier, in August 1909, Constable JT Campbell had visited Liveringa with his offsiders on station patrol. Percy Rose informed him that there were two female and three male 'half-caste' children between the ages of five and fourteen on Liveringa. One was his ten-year-old son, Yoolya Fraser.

Campbell camped at a spot called Police Camp alongside a creek near the Grant Range just 2 kilometres west of the

Liveringa homestead. The picturesque range with craggy outcrops and spinifex-coated terrain slides through the land-scape, casting a myriad of colours far and wide at dusk over the camp where Aboriginal prisoners were once held up en route to Derby. Under instructions from the District Officer in Broome, he returned in October 1909 to take the children.

An early afternoon storm brewed that hot and humid day as a young Yoolya ran around helping chase chooks into their yard when Campbell, with Fraser and Rose, arrived at the camp. Walter Fraser did his best to console a tearful and confused young boy and his mum when he told them that Yoolya must leave now and go with the police to Derby. Yoolya, he said, was going by boat to a place a long way up from Derby to work and live with good people. Fraser assured her that everything would be OK – the boy would be in safe hands. Stumpy never saw her son again.

It was a slow, jarring 120-kilometre trip by horse and dray over bush tracks to Derby, where Grampa met eight other 'half-caste' boys who had been taken from their families in similar fashion. They were all destined to travel on the SS *Koombana* to Pago, the very same ship that had taken Granny away from Derby a few months earlier. The boys' travel was arranged by the Protector of Aborigines office in Perth, then under Charles Frederick Gale. The Adelaide Steamship Company's shipping agents, Forrest, Emmanuel and Co, were asked to divert the ship to Drysdale River on its way to Wyndham. On 11 November 1909 they responded,

> *Dear Sir – We have yours of the 10th. Inst. And note that you desire the steamer 'Koombana' on her voyage from Derby to Wyndham, December trip, to call in at Drysdale Mission to land*

some half dozen half-caste boys, the arrangement being that they
pay ordinary schedule fares, and the sum of £10 for the deviation.

On 20 December the SS *Koombana* set sail for Drysdale River with stores, thirty sheep and its young human cargo. The boys had never been to the coast before, let alone travelled on an ocean-going vessel. The journey was rough. It was the build-up to the cyclone season and forceful winds buffeted the ship. As the skipper negotiated increasing swells, the boys suffered dreadful seasickness. Once their ordeal was over, they settled into their new home, an evolving Benedictine mission where they were baptised and Grampa was named 'Fulgentius' after Abbot Fulgentius Torres.

Three years later, on 20 March 1912, almost to the day from when it had started servicing ports on the northwest coast, the SS *Koombana* met its ultimate fate. The ship that had taken my grandparents away from Derby, and had transported our people to prisons away from their homelands, vanished. The elegant, ultra-modern steamship heading north disappeared off the coast of Port Hedland in a cyclone. Its crew and passengers were lost and never found.

———

At Pago, the missionaries endured an isolated existence. Only once a year did a lugger bring supplies and news from New Norcia. Nonetheless, they tried desperately to entice the 'blacks' into their haven, with the 'half-caste' boys proving to be the ideal support they needed. Together they walked in the bush, hanging clothes on shrubs for the bush people while praying fervently for the success of their mission.

Two years after the boys arrived, Abbot Torres, who was also the Catholic Bishop and Administrator of the Kimberley, wrote to the Chief Protector of Aborigines assuring him that he had 'great hope for the future of this new mission'. In a letter dated 30 June 1911 he claimed,

When the treacherous and blood-thirsty natives yield to the constancy and undaunted bravery of the Fathers and Brothers, the new establishment will be in a position to stand and support a good number of them ... The half-caste boys sent by the Government two years ago are doing very well.

The Abbot continued to be impressed with the boys and in his 1913 report to the Protector he sang their praises, 'The boys we have show a decided willingness and eagerness for assisting in everything that has been done ... these boys are very active, intelligent, give no trouble whatever and are much attached to the priests.' The Benedictine's prayers to bring the Kwini and Kulari into their mission were eventually answered, but not before an attack on 27 September 1913 in which Father Alcade almost died.

Suspicious of the missionaries and never understanding why they persisted in staying in their country uninvited, 103 men and women hid spears in the grass before approaching the monks. They appeared friendly enough, as they waited for a signal to attack. Following a loud cry, spears rained in on the unsuspecting missionaries and Fr Alcade and Brother Vincent were severely bludgeoned. Fearing for their lives, it was a quick-thinking fourteen-year-old Fulgentius who saved them. He ran to Alcade's room, found a gun and fired it into the air, sending the attackers retreating into the bush. Alcade lay ill for several months until he was able to return to New Norcia for proper care. Br Vincent remained at the mission.

Drysdale River Mission. State Library of Western Australia (b5321999_28)

Grampa grew into a selfless young man who had little choice but to abide by the Benedictine's idea of reform as he went about converting the local people to Catholicism. The monks had become his surrogate family.

It wasn't long before he reached a marriageable age but there was a problem, according to the new Chief Protector of Aborigines, Auber Octavius Neville. At Pago, all the women were black. Under Neville's way of thinking, black women were undesirable brides for men of 'mixed descent'. He believed in eugenics – the theory that the human race could be improved by controlled breeding. Before the arrival of westerners, Australia's first peoples were already living a sophisticated, disease-free lifestyle that had evolved over thousands of years with no 'contamination' from Europeans. Now Neville's view was that an Aryan race (to which he himself belonged) was the standard to which all other races should aspire. Therefore, as a 'mixed-descent' man, Grampa was only allowed to marry a woman of the same complexion as himself or lighter. Furthermore, the Chief Protector was convinced that black-skinned people were dying out.

In 1918 Grampa and the other 'half-caste' men were sent to Beagle Bay to find wives. He was given work in the mission bakery and he soon met a young woman who worked in the convent. A good-looking, petite woman with high cheekbones, my Granny had a mischievous, infectious grin. He was attracted to her immediately and, with the approval of the missionaries, their courtship began.

The church that Granny had helped gather shells to build was completed in 1918 and named the Sacred Heart, in time for her marriage the following year. Before their wedding, Grampa wrote to the monks at New Norcia asking about them by name and reminding them of the good times they enjoyed together at Pago. He asked the monks for help with his wedding plans, signing off with,

> *Please my Lord I ask you if you can sent to me a per of suite for my married day. I will be very pleased and thankfull for your great kindness. I think with the help of God I will get married after Easter, so please sent it to me for the day? and some holy pictures and one rosary bead. I think that's all for this time. Goodbye may Gods blessing upon you. As I remains yours faithfully Child in J.C. Fulgentius Eulla.*

It was barrgana (winter) time on 5 August 1919. A time of year when eerie fogs rose above the nearby lakes then drifted across the mission, nudged on by dry, easterly winds as the newlyweds walked back down the aisle of the Beagle Bay church followed by their attendants, Mary Underwood and Carmel Marshall. My grandparents looked dapper in attire provided by the missionaries. The Beagle Bay mob celebrated their marriage in good old European style – wedding cake, smorgasbord and singing and dancing. They were allocated a cottage built from handmade mud bricks with a thatched roof and large shutters in the 'colony'. Their home blended in with similar cottages on sandy soil and low grass, away from the dormitory and the school. They paid rent but finding paid work was never easy.

The following year the first of their children arrived: Katie – my mother. Delivered by Aboriginal midwives in her parents' cottage on 24 November 1920, she was christened 'Mary Catherine' on the very same day. In fact, every female born on the mission between 1919 and 1940 was christened Mary. Over the next twenty years Granny gave birth to nine babies – one did not survive. Unlike their parents, the Fraser children were born into an institutionalised life. A Western lifestyle was imposed on them that systematically broke down their Aboriginal beliefs, their languages and their customs. My Nigena family's identity was severely threatened as they were forced into a different way of living.

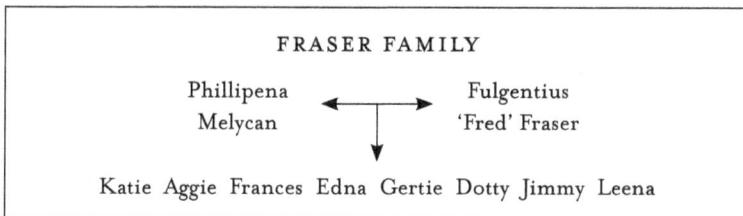

FRASER FAMILY

| Phillipena | | Fulgentius |
| Melycan | ⟵——⟶ | 'Fred' Fraser |

Katie Aggie Frances Edna Gertie Dotty Jimmy Leena

Granny was pregnant with her second child in 1923 when Grampa helped her and their little girl aboard the mission lugger in Broome, headed for Pago. He was taking them 'home'. Like others before her, travelling through the Buccaneer Archipelago on a small vessel terrified the young Katie, despite the beauty of the coastline with its spectacular rocky outcrops and waterfalls. Such magnificent scenery was barely noticed in 1923 by people who were forced to live in a foreign country, let alone a small child. The lugger rocked and swayed as it climbed high waves and dodged huge whirlpools on its way to Joseph Bonaparte Gulf and into the mouth of the Drysdale River. Mum never forgot those dreadful journeys, so sick she cried and begged her parents to never take her on a boat ever again.

At Pago the family moved into a small, comfortable cottage and Grampa re-engaged with his evangelistic work while Granny joined other 'mixed-descent' women to teach the local women domestic chores. Their second daughter arrived on 4 January 1924 and she was baptised Agnes Eulla. Benedict Mondal and Cecelia Jimbery, friends of my grandparents, stood as her godparents. She became known as 'Aggie' and she was their only daughter not to be named Mary. Moreover, she was the only Fraser sibling not born at Beagle Bay. The Drysdale River families developed strong bonds while remaining subservient to and reliant on the missionaries. Nonetheless, they enjoyed their pastimes together, fishing from the beach and in the rivers. Slapping the water with tree branches, the women and children chased fish into the shallows while the men stood on the rocks and speared the fish as they fled by.

However before too long, Granny and Grampa along with

Benedict and Cecelia were back in Beagle Bay. Cecelia had become frightened and fearful, convinced even, that she was going to be killed by the local people at Pago. Granny too was worried after witnessing a violent attack on a woman by her male companion, so Grampa and Benedict agreed that it was best for their families to leave.

'Mixed-descent' families, Drysdale River Mission, 1924. Source unknown

At Beagle Bay they were again allocated a cottage in the colony. But within five years of their return the mission was struggling and not able to support its people. Granny and Grampa's ability to pay rent became difficult and even more so when, by the mid-1930s, Granny had given birth to four more Marys – Frances, Edna, Gertrude and Dorothy. Edna as a young girl had quizzed her mum about the night she was born on 21 June 1928, right on winter solstice, the longest and coldest night that Granny ever remembered. Aboriginal midwives delivered Edna and the nuns brought Granny warm milk and soup. In that swampy country it was so cold that even the billycans of water the family kept in the cottage had partially turned to ice.

Grampa, meanwhile, knew that he had little choice but to find work outside the mission so he wrote to the abbot asking if he could return with his brood to Pago. His request was turned down, probably for the same reason that Beagle Bay could no longer support families. There was no money. So began a slow exodus of people from the mission. In 1930 Grampa alone moved away. Over the next ten years he worked as a stockman on northwest pastoral stations, including two years at Ethel Creek Station, 80 kilometres north of Mount Newman in the Pilbara.

———

From the early 1900s Kimberley people were being affected by introduced diseases, in particular, leprosy (Hansen's Disease). It had spread to northern Australia and those affected, and even some who weren't but were assumed to have the disease, were quarantined. Almost any gudia could examine an Aboriginal person to decide whether they had an infectious disease. Forced to leave the missions and stations, Derby patients were treated in an improvised 'native' hospital that was also the government residency building. Gazetted as a quarantine reserve in 1910, the site was in a sparsely vegetated area among the mangroves. The idea that the people there, mostly Aboriginal, had leprosy caused agitation in Derby, so in 1924, a separate hospital for gudias was built, while the leper patients remained in the old building. But within a year they were transferred and dumped at Cossack, 700 kilometres south of Derby. The Derby hospital was then burned to the ground to prevent the disease spreading. Ten years later inmates were relocated, yet again, this time from Cossack to an island off the Northern Territory, until the government acknowledged a specialist hospital was needed in the Kimberley.

In 1936 a leprosarium was established at Bungarun, 16 kilometres north of Derby, forcing the Kimberley patients to be relocated yet again – this time from the Northern Territory. It was the St John of God sisters who came to care for those affected, but for Muninga, who was still living in Derby and still pining for her daughter, their arrival was serendipitous. She wondered if they were the people in white that she had been told about. Regardless, she attached herself to them despite not having leprosy. In the sisters she found a symbolic link to her daughter and the grandchildren she never knew.

The sisters gave Muninga work and food at their lazaret. Mother Gertrude Green, who was in charge, cared for her though Muninga probably lived in the bush between Bungarun and Derby. In return, she did odd jobs for the sisters – cleaning and raking leaves, just like she had done for Quan Sing all those years ago. Mother Gertrude baptised my great-granny and called her Lucy. Through the St John of God sisters, Lucy Muninga found much-needed solace.

Nygumi, meanwhile, had moved on from Yeeda after the girls were taken. He worked as a cook in Broome hotels and at some point was a cook on the ship MV *Kangaroo*. He remained connected with his Aboriginal family through both Granny and Gypsy and he stayed in contact with his relatives in India (now Pakistan).

———

Like other Aboriginal stockmen, my Grampa played an important role as a drover delivering stock to southern markets during the 1930s. It is how he supported his family at Beagle Bay – earning about £1 a day. The work kept him away for months on end. Unlike gudia stockmen, Aboriginal people's full names seldom appear in the literature. Thankfully, my aunties' childhood memories capture snippets about their father. Their oral histories complement the white drovers' tales, especially those of Jim Freeth, who managed droving plants on the same routes down to Meekatharra during the same period as Grampa.

Quite a few contractors existed in the day. A plant consisted of a dozen or so stockmen, comprising mostly blackfullas, an Aboriginal woman (as cook or horsetailer) and a couple of gudia. Some plants had up to forty workhorses and a few camels. The horses were rotated each day. At night they were hobbled so they could feed while the stockmen took shifts watching the stock. A dray carried all the necessary equipment – tools, saddles, medicine chest, swags and stores.

At the beginning of a muster south, cattle came under the scrutiny of a stock inspector and a veterinary surgeon from the Agriculture Department. Tested for 'pluro pneumonic', a lung disease found in cattle, blood samples were sent to Perth by air. The all clear, or otherwise, was sent back via telegram.

On arrival at Meekatharra the stock was transferred by train to Geraldton, to the Midland saleyards or to Robbs Jetty in

Fremantle. The work was labour intensive and relentless. Droving a 'lift' of 700 head from Anna Plains to Meekatharra, the plant covered about 10 kilometres a day, mustering and cracking the whip along the 960-kilometre stock route. The long muster took four months. Cattle were watered every 30 kilometres or so, generally at government-installed wells since rivers ran dry even during the winter. I was impressed by the way in which droving teams agreed to stagger their mob, leaving enough distance between herds to allow for soaks to replenish the wells before the next mob arrived. By comparison, the return journey took the droving plant six weeks.

To a lesser degree sheep were also brought down the inland routes, up to 7,000 head at a time. But sheep musters appear to have been less successful because of diseases like 'pink eye', a condition that causes blindness and a thiamine deficiency resulting in brain malfunction – the sheep go crazy. Added to this, the long trudge for smaller animals would have had its drawbacks.

The first consignment to Meekatharra in 1934 arrived in good nick, despite some feeding issues and lack of water from the government wells close to journey's end. Nonetheless, that consignment sold for a good price at Meekatharra and in Midland.

At one time, Grampa was away droving for nearly three years. It was during this time that he had another daughter, Clare, who was raised by her mother in the Gascoyne region. Granny and Clare's Beagle Bay siblings embraced their sister and we remain close to her children, our first cousins.

Grampa stayed in contact with the Benedictines. On one journey, keen to see Fr Alcade again, he left his droving plant at Meekatharra and rode 600 kilometres southwest to New

Norcia. Their mutual affection had not faded and the monks held him in high esteem. Now, sixteen years later, they were only too happy to see Fulgentius again – he had become part of folklore among the Benedictines for saving Alcade's life. The two were often seen together walking in the monastery grounds reminiscing about their Pago days.

Fr Alcade and
Br Vincent,
New Norcia, 1935.
Source unknown

When Grampa received a telegram from his boss asking him to hurry back to Meekatharra as there was much work to do, he left without further ado. The monks extolled one of their favourite 'half-caste' boys in New Norcia's St Ildephonsus College magazine in 1930: 'In his lonely rides by ridge and river, by creek and pool, across mountains, plains and valleys, we wish him every happiness his stout, brave heart deserves.'

During his time off Grampa headed home to Beagle Bay. After travelling on the mission supply boat from Broome to the bay, he continued his journey on the stores cart. As he neared the mission, he laughed aloud. He could hear his children yelling in the distance even before he saw them, running barefoot along the dirt track. They had got wind that 'Poppa', as they called him, was coming home. He always brought goodies. Big tins of lollies and fancy biscuits and little bloomers and dresses that they delighted in. They were in their glory. But soon work called and he was gone. Just like when he arrived, they all cried again.

During this time, Granny was reunited with her mother. The nuns arranged a meeting at the One Mile Camp next to the main road into Broome and Granny took the children to meet her. Not knowing what to expect and with curious anticipation, the kids sat on a canvas spread on the ground under the coolness of a tree as they watched the meeting unfold. The two women were finally reunited, holding each other for a long while and sobbing uncontrollably. Muninga and Granny's last memory of one another was vivid, reaching back thirty years to when they were torn apart.

Loud wailing erupted from the onlookers. Everyone wept openly with rousing compassion. That moment in time had an everlasting impact on my mother and her sisters Aggie and Edna. Mum never forgot the numbness she felt that day. She would mention it whenever we visited Broome. Aggie, too, when visiting Broome with her family would point and say, 'That's where we were,' as they drove past the One Mile Camp.

While Granny and her children lived in Beagle Bay, Nygumi was for some time with Gypsy and her two children in Broome, where he continued to practise his Muslim faith. He cut sandalwood to make joss sticks and he tended the perpetual light in the mosque. A thoughtful man and in keeping with his attitude towards Nigena people's customs, he respected Catholic beliefs too. Yet he forbade his Christian family to enter the mosque.

———

Nygumi was in his mid-fifties when arthritis began spreading to his joints – very likely the result of having been a pearl-shell diver – and he became less mobile. He went to live with Granny at Beagle Bay where she could care for him. His old friend Eddy Yedewarra still lived in the humpies, and the two were happy to be in each other's company again.

With Grampa away, Granny cherished her time with her kids, making toys and ragdolls that the girls filled with sand, then when they were absorbed by the mission milieu, she worked in the convent. The siblings hold precious memories of their mission days – it was all they knew. Even Mum claimed that her days at Beagle Bay were the happiest of her life.

From the time she was six, my mother lived in the dormitory where some of the older girls looked after the children, including Grace Beasley Martin. Gracie had been taken from the Ord River region herself and, with husband Vince Martin, she had been at Drysdale River at the same time as Granny and Grampa. She was the closest Mum had to a real mother in the dormitory. The two always remained close.

As the family grew, Aggie joined Mum in the dormitory. The small cottage in the colony wasn't big enough for all of them. Nevertheless, the family managed. Granny and Grampa slept in the middle room with baby Dottie, while Frances, Edna and Gertie slept head to toe in a large double bed on a hay-filled mattress. Nygumi had a separate room. They had only a bare minimum of eating utensils since food was prepared and served from the mission's kitchen, though the children usually ate in the dining room.

The dormitory atmosphere was pleasant enough. The kids dressed in clean clothes and the bigger ones had their own bed, white sheets and blankets, while the littlies slept on the floor. Sometimes during their afternoon rest, they sat on the beds with the hum of mission activities drifting through the thin lace curtains. There, they listened to stories of far-off places from the Irish nuns. The children were disciplined but never mistreated, nor stopped from visiting their parents. Staying in the dormitory meant that the younger Fraser siblings were with Katie. But they could go home whenever they wanted to. 'Go on. You can sleep with your parents if you want to. Or stay with Katie in the dormitory,' a nun gestured towards the colony.

Chores were carried out every day by the children. They helped to hand out rations of bread, tea, jam, meat and vegetables to the adults, who in turn helped themselves to flour and sugar from the store. Early each morning the kids rose to milk the cows and goats, prepare the ovens and set the dining rooms before heading off to mass, then breakfast, then school. Jobs rotated weekly, working in the convent kitchen, in the dining room, cleaning the church and helping in the vegetable garden.

Aggie was an offsider to her friend Laura Booty in the kitchen but best of all she liked working outdoors with Brother John and Brother Matt in the sugar plantation. She helped till the paddocks with bullocks, pushing grass through the plough and even washing the friendly bullocks.

Side by side girls and boys marched into class each morning singing renditions of 'The Men of Harlech' and other British tunes. With angelic voices they harmonised favourites 'Whispering Hope' and 'Irish Eyes'. Years later we occasionally heard Mum and her sisters harmonising those songs together. Despite their basic schooling, the children developed fine handwriting styles, as did my Granny.

Prayer was an integral part of mission life and evenings were for devotion. Almost everyone headed into the church for Benediction before going outside for Rosary. They gathered around big, flickering campfires, loudly chanting the rosary with the kids racing through it so they could go and play before bedtime at eight o'clock. Prayer wasn't just an entrenched practice among the mission folk. It was socially rewarding. Even though a decree of the missionaries, prayer brought people together – it ensured the forming of relationships. So tight was that bonding that today descendants are confused about who is related to who. Many embrace and claim one another as relatives, as kinship knowledges handed down from families in the humpies became confused under Western systems.

After Sunday mass, mission folk often walked the 10 kilometres to the bay for a picnic, sometimes staying overnight. During holiday times Nygumi took his grandchildren camping for up to two weeks in bush along the beach. He relished being with them and they with him. When he became so crippled that he could no longer walk, his grandchildren helped him around the cottage. Rearranging his arthritic-ridden legs, five-year-old Edna lifted them into a more comfortable position and brought him food and water. That was her job. He was a jovial character. Joining in with the kids as they played chasey through the cottage, he would use his walking stick to trip up the child who was winning because he felt sorry for the slower ones. Nygumi's sisters sent saris from India for the grandkids, but they weren't allowed to wear them because they weren't mission supplied – or perhaps because they weren't European attire. Nygumi became a Catholic in 1933 and an almost fanatic one at that, crawling to church when his mission mates weren't around to help him hobble there. Three years later he died. He was laid to rest in the Beagle Bay cemetery.

Edna, Leena, Aggie and Shelley (rear) at Nygumi's grave, Beagle Bay Mission, 2015 © Kylie Gibson, photographer

When Muninga died in 1938 in Derby, Sr Gertrude travelled to Beagle Bay with the news. Perhaps because of her compassion for mothers of stolen children, she wanted to reassure Granny that her mother was now at peace in heaven. As the nun from Derby approached their cottage, the children playing outside sensed something had happened and they ran to tell their mother.

Granny cried and her children cried with her. Sr Gertrude had wanted her to know that Lucy Muninga was buried just over the cemetery fence at Bungarun – outside the graveyard because she wasn't a leprosy patient. After clearly explaining where the grave was, the nun returned to Bungarun. Over the years, Granny made sure that her children knew the exact spot so that one day they might honour their grandmother, Lucy Muninga, by laying a headstone over her grave. Which they did in 2015.

Aggie, Leena and Edna at Muninga's grave, Bungarun, 2015 © Kylie Gibson, photographer

It was the late 1930s when Bishop Otto Raible, the Administrator Apostolic of the Vicariate for the Kimberley, hoped some Beagle Bay boys might be prepared to become priests. He was disappointed. They had no inclination. So he turned his attention to the girls and this time he was not disappointed. His spirits lifted as young women showed a keen interest. He immediately set about preparing a report for the Mother General of the St John of God sisters in Wexford, Ireland, outlining his objectives and explaining that the Aboriginal nuns' main role would be to evangelise their own people. With his plan approved, Raible set the wheels in motion.

Wanting to be certain the girls were genuine, the bishop held a retreat. Twenty-seven, my mother included, showed great fervour and devotion according to the bishop. He had asked them to write down any concerns and place them in a question box. Given that the only nuns they knew were white European women, it is no surprise that the most asked question was whether it was possible for a 'native or half-caste girl' to be a nun. He reassured them that the colour of their skin was no barrier. Satisfied that they were sincere, the bishop made application to the Holy See, the Pope in Rome, asking permission to start a convent just for Aboriginal women. With approval gained, he began establishing what became colloquially known as 'the black convent'.

My mother realised that, living where career opportunities were nil, doing something with apparent status was sure worth thinking about. Should she give it a go? She talked it over with her parents. They assured her that it was her choice; there was no pressure from them if she wanted to be a nun. She had their unconditional support. With that my mother formally applied along with six other aspirants. Mum was already seventeen in January 1939 when she entered formal religious life with three others, Vera Dann, Biddy Kelly and Lucy Albert. They were the first to join the Sisters of Our Lady, Queen of the Apostles Convent for Aboriginal postulants at Beagle Bay. All met the eligibility criteria laid out in the Rules of the Society of Native Sisters, and Mum became Sister Mary Agnes.

> Rule 1: Any Catholic girl of at least one half of Aboriginal blood can be admitted if she has the right intention, is bodily and mentally fitted for missionary work and is of a sociable disposition.

However, the young women were not prepared for such strict discipline. Cloistral life was challenging:

> Rule 7: The novices will not speak to anyone outside the convent except what their various duties require. They can receive visitors once a month.

The novitiates were kept busy and trained in domestic work of every description. They washed the old priests' clothes and the linen, boiling them in large coppers, and they learned how to cook. Mum taught in the school and she helped in the health clinic. Together with the white nuns she visited the colony to administer first aid and to dispense medicines. She learned to crochet, attaching her handiwork to the hem of the altar cloth, and she learned to play the piano. Confined to the convent, Mum looked forward to the family's monthly visits and they were only too happy to see her. The younger ones were always looking out for her around the mission, in the convent yard and at church. Mum did embrace her religious commitments, but cracks began to appear. In her own mind, she questioned why she wasn't allowed to talk to her family. It was unreasonable to be expected to shun them. She found that she couldn't obey Rule 7. Her younger siblings missed her closeness, her parents missed her, and she missed the family.

Biddy Kelly, Vera Dann, Bishop Raible, Lucy Albert, Katie Fraser at Beagle Bay Mission, 1939. Source unknown

Grampa was away droving when an opportunity came his way in 1940 to move back closer to his Nigena homelands and to his family. Called 'Fred' by his contemporaries, he started working as a sheep overseer at Myroodah, a one-million-acre pastoral property south of the Mardoowarra. Granny and the family would eventually join him. Their exodus from the mission seriously affected my mother, who remained in the 'black' convent.

Left to right: Aggie, Edna, Granny holding Leena, Dottie, Gertie holding Jimmy, Katie and Frances, Beagle Bay Mission, 1940. Source unknown

CHAPTER 2

A change of direction

*Thirty-five years after being removed to Drysdale River
Mission, my Grampa returned to his homeland*

Running through Myroodah Station is the upper section
of the Mardoowarra. Its soft, black topsoil surrounded by
white gums reaches out to touch the great walmarda (desert).
Rocky outcrops peer searchingly into the distance over low
spinifex, glimpsing an occasional glistening jila (waterhole) as
it puffs a shimmering haze towards the midday sun. This is the
Great Sandy Desert, which several Aboriginal homelands are
connected to.

Harold Godbehear, the station's manager, told his new
overseer that it would take twelve months for a hut to be ready
at the Currigan sheep camp. It is where Grampa would live
with his family. On hearing this, Granny took the children
from the mission to Broome to live while waiting for the hut
to be completed. She did, however, return to Beagle Bay for the
birth of her two youngest, Jimmy in August 1939 and Leena in
November 1940. When the time came to leave for Currigan,

Granny settled Edna, aged twelve, and Gertie, ten, with my mother in the black convent at Beagle Bay to continue their schooling, while everyone else moved away. Edna enjoyed being in the convent despite not aspiring to become a nun. She just enjoyed the company of her friends and she liked to dress in pretty little veils and habits. Yet she missed her parents and her siblings terribly.

Grampa, meanwhile, was keen to improve life for his family, under Western systems, so he decided to apply for an exemption from the *Native Administration Act 1936* (WA). That way, he reasoned, they would all be better off because they could live as gudia did rather than being controlled by them. He wasn't sure how to apply so he asked Walter Fraser, who happened to be working at Myroodah, to find out.

The old man hit an early snag since he hardly knew his stepson, let alone Grampa's family. When questioned by Mr Bray from the Department of Native Affairs, Fraser didn't even know his daughter-in-law's first or last names. Neither did he know the name of his son's daughter, the one who was a nun in the convent at Beagle Bay. Furthermore, Granny and the children didn't know him. Fraser had never acquainted himself with Grampa's family. Surely, if he was the real father, he would have shown some interest in his grandchildren.

As I pored over my grandparents' native welfare file I cringed, even more than when I read Mum's personal file. Condescending words like 'boy' and 'type' are rife in the documentation. Bray instructed Walter Fraser to go and tell his son that he must apply by himself, in his own handwriting. Furthermore, he warned, 'If he can't write then he should ask

someone who can. That being the case, the boy must then sign
the application with his '"mark" in the presence of a responsible
witness.' In the letter dated 11 October 1940, Bray continued,
'Mr Fraser, please ensure the family understands that they must
reject their Aboriginality and they must agree to certain conditions. Stress to them, that they must not mix with Aboriginal
people and they should behave in a civilised way.'

With that Fraser left and Bray set about looking for a file on
Brumby, Grampa's birth mother. Her file would prove once and
for all, he decided, whether Fred Fraser was indeed married to a
'half-caste'. But he couldn't find any file. So he sent Walter Fraser
a message, threatening that if his son was living in a conjugal
relationship with a 'native' of the opposite sex, he would not get
an exemption.

My Grampa could write. Moreover, he was living in a manner
that satisfied gudia as he set about applying for an exemption for
his family shortly before the birth of his youngest child, Leena.

Harold Godbehear provided a reference verifying that Fred
Fraser, 'Is a very good type and quite worthy of the privilege',
while Mr R Bell, the manager of Ellendale Station, stated,
'I have known the boy for the last 35 years and I have known
him to be always of a good character, a good trustworthy and a
well behaved man.' Even the Derby police considered Grampa
a decent 'type' of 'half-caste' who was no trouble, while some
Derby townsfolk claimed he was of quiet disposition and clean
habits. The Fraser family's exemption application was officially
recognised in March 1941. Grampa's endorsement came with a
stern warning via the Derby police sergeant, who was a protector
of 'natives', 'would you please warn Fraser that retention of this

privilege will rest wholly and solely upon his future actions and conduct. He must live according to white standards and cease forthwith all associations with natives at law.'

Department of Native Affairs, Fulgentius Fraser 'Personal file' (945/40, DAA, 1940)

Aggie at seventeen years of age became Myroodah's chief cook while Frances, just fifteen, became a housemaid. Both worked for Mrs Godbehear at the homestead, 48 kilometres from Currigan, earning a few shillings. A striking teenager, Aggie's long, shiny black hair topped a slim physique and, at 165 centimetres, she stood tall against her sisters. Her strong jawline resembled Grampa's. She had a serious demeanour – a focused and determined young woman. Like all the Fraser siblings, my aunty was a force to be reckoned with. A fast learner, she cooked meals for up to seventeen people – Aboriginal and gudia. She baked bread and roasts and she cooked corned beef complemented with a tasty selection of vegetables from the station's gardens. On weekends the girls joined the mob in the camp by the river where about fifteen people lived and they headed to Currigan whenever they could.

Working for Mrs Godbehear was tough, and the girls missed the congeniality and support of the family. After a couple of years, restless and fed up, they decided they had been there too long, as Aggie confided in her father. Mr Godbehear, she told him, was good-natured enough but Mrs Godbehear was a different story. Their relationship had become strained, to a point where Aggie tipped flour over Mrs Godbehear's head. Quickly packing their few possessions, the girls left.

They knew that friends from Beagle Bay, Tom Puertollano and Jerome Manado, were working in a nearby paddock putting up a windmill so they headed there. The two men were surprised to see the girls appear out of the bush. They immediately sensed something was wrong when they suddenly hid. Harold Godbehear was hot on their heels and Tom and Jerome assured him that they hadn't seen the two. Aggie proudly boasted to me about their escape tactics, 'He didn't find us. We saw him, but we didn't walk on the road, just the spinifex and we hid under kungerberry tree. I heard Mr Godbehear saying, "Can you see tracks?" and the Aboriginal boy saying, "No boss, no boss". The whole family soon left Myroodah.

They moved to Sheep Camp, an outstation on Hill Station north of Broome owned by Streeter and Male that had previously been managed by Harry and Maude Denham. The family sometimes called it Denham Station. A few people from the mission worked there too, especially during shearing time. Grampa taught his children to round up sheep, tally the flock, separate and class wool, and press fleeces into large wool bales. A shearing team travelled the West Kimberley circuit, staying at Hill Station for a week or two before moving on to the next contract, leaving the station hands to shear the stragglers. With bales piled high on his Chevrolet truck, Tom Puertollano delivered the wool to the Broome port. By now, he and Aggie had begun a relationship.

Frances, Granny, Leena, Jimmy and Aggie. Sheep Camp, Hill Station, early 1940s.
Source unknown

In the early 1940s northern Australia was feeling the effects of WWII, which much of Europe had been drawn into. Australia joined in. As the war intensified in the region following the bombing of Broome by the Japanese on 3 March 1942, the Australian Air Force took over the Broome orphanage as its base and Aboriginal people were evacuated to missions on the Dampier Peninsula. The Fraser kids were relocated to Beagle Bay, where they stayed until the war ended. Adults made their own way to the missions and Aggie, who had been working for Magistrate Cowan and his wife in Broome, hitched a ride with Laura Booty on a truck loaded with orphanage kids. Tom, too, made his way back to the mission.

The orphanage kids were housed in the 'black convent' as the influx of people stretched the mission's domestic capacity. To cope, a new wing was added to the hospital and a school was built. More problems confronted the missionaries when the German Pallottines were considered a security risk by the Australian government and sent off to internment camps in Alice Springs, causing a staff shortage. In fact, anyone from any country that was considered to even loosely have sympathies with Hitler's Germany was interned. This left the nuns to run the mission, supported by the 'native' sisters.

The war had little effect on Aggie and Tom's relationship. It blossomed and they set a wedding date for 30 January 1943. The nuns enthusiastically took on the role of wedding planners. They prepared the food, decorated the school for the reception and made a three-tiered wedding cake. Aggie's beautiful lace and sequin-lined dress was the creation of Lilly Puertollano, Tom's sister. With the Sacred Heart Church packed and all the family there, Grampa proudly walked his secondborn down the aisle. The first wedding, he mused to himself, of potentially another five daughters since one daughter would become a nun. In all likelihood he was quietly pleased that Aggie's suitor was none other than the handsome and affable Tom Puertollano. Monica and Susie Dolby were her bridesmaids while the popular Bishop Raible, at Aggie's request, blissfully consecrated their wedding vows.

*Tom and Aggie
Puertollano,
Beagle Bay,
30 January 1943.
Source unknown*

Granny and Grampa had an extra passenger on their way back to Sheep Camp – Edna. She had been excited and emotional to see them arrive in Pop's little motorcar for the wedding, and she wasn't about to let them leave her behind. 'Once I saw them,' she admitted to me, 'I didn't want to stay in the convent anymore.'

To everyone's excitement, Grampa received a letter from the manager of Liveringa, Kim Rose, offering him a job as an overseer – right in the heart of his Nigena homelands. A shiver ran down his spine. Kim was the nephew of Percy Rose, his biological father. Unable to contain his excitement, he called to Edna and showed her the letter. As Edna read it out Granny felt a lump in her throat and she looked at Grampa admiringly. She knew what a valued stockman her husband was. With her backing, it wasn't hard for him to make a decision straight away: he was going home.

Grampa was to be paid £10 a week, unlike the £5 he earned with Streeter and Male and a promise of accommodation for the family, yet to be built. For the time being, he settled the family into a rented house in Derby owned by their friend, Granny Griffiths. He then left for Willumbah, one of Liveringa's sheep camps. Willumbah, meaning big floods, is nestled right on the edge of the Mardoowarra floodplains a few kilometres north of the Liveringa homestead. Thirty-five years after being removed to Drysdale River Mission, Grampa returned to his Nigena homelands. Home to his full-descent family, who were still there, defying the predictions of white Australians like AO Neville, the Chief Protector of Aborigines.

———

Tom and Aggie moved on from Beagle Bay in 1943, spending time at Yeeda Station before relocating to Derby, closer to Granny and the children. Tom continued working on pastoral properties while Aggie, now pregnant, was a welcome support to Granny and the little ones, Dottie, Jimmy and Leena. Both Edna and Frances found work in Derby that year, while Gertie stayed on with Mum at Beagle Bay. Whenever she could, Granny took the kids out to Willumbah.

Life in town was different to the mission. The Fraser siblings hadn't learned to survive outside of an institutionalised life, other than to be domestics and labourers for gudia people, which they accepted to be their calling in life once they left the mission. They had no idea what racism or discrimination meant. It wasn't until they went to live in towns that they noticed gudia reacted differently to them. That non-Aboriginal people would consider them inferior was a shock. Quite a few 'mixed-descent' people even claimed not to be Aboriginal and ostracised their own countrimin. Under laws that were hell-bent on assimilating Aboriginal peoples, it is little wonder they kept quiet about who they really were. As for the Frasers, it never entered their heads to deny their Aboriginality, yet they always defended the missionaries' paternalistic approach to them. Their gudia mission protectors could do no wrong in their eyes.

Frances worked as a domestic at the Club Hotel and Edna landed her first job at the Derby Post Office, earning £2.10 a week. Competent in English and with stylish handwriting, she penned telegrams then delivered them on pushbike around the town. She also operated the tiny switchboard. At just fifteen Edna was the first Aboriginal female to ever work in the Derby Post Office, where she stayed until 1947. She was eligible for the job not only because of her skills but because she had an exemption from the *Native Administration Act*, thanks to Grampa. On weekends she helped Frances at the Club Hotel, polishing cutlery and carrying out general kitchen duties.

My mother's experiences as a novitiate remain vague and she rarely talked about her time in the 'black convent'. Perhaps by her applying for an exemption in 1943 she was pre-empting her 1946 departure, even though mission residents were not eligible for exemptions. It was considered unnecessary for them. An exemption was only ever given to people who were deemed ready to leave a mission or a reserve – those who were ready to 'better themselves'. People eligible to leave the mission were considered capable of showing respect to their new employers and it was assumed they had the ability to save money, despite never having had any on the mission. Mum, on the other hand, was expected to be a God-abiding nun for the rest of her life, so she needn't worry about applying.

Yet she applied. She argued that because she was considered to be a respectful human being by the Catholic fraternity, she should also be regarded as such by the government. Her closing comments in her application reflect her uneasiness at being confined to the convent,

> *I do think that my interests are now sufficiently protected by the religious society to which I belong and which is under the special protectorate of His Lordship, Bishop Raible. It is mainly for this reason that I apply for an exemption from the Native Administration Act. Yours faithfully, Sister M. Agnes Fraser. (14 April 1943)*

But she and her contemporaries would always be seen as lesser children of God, and she knew it. In a letter to the Honourable Minister for the North West, the Commissioner of Native Affairs claimed that young novitiates' vows were 'in no way comparable to those taken by the members of the Order of St. John of God'. Regardless, Mum was approved for an exemption.

Laws specifically for Aboriginal peoples continued to be tinkered with on a regular basis across Australia. Gudia were good at that – changing their minds since they believed they knew what was best for our mob. In 1944 the state law was amended again. Aboriginals in Western Australia became eligible to apply to be an Australian citizen, despite their 80,000+ year heritage as Australia's first peoples. Citizenship superseded an exemption. But like all the previous laws, the new law was offensive. The applicant still had to prove they were not diseased with leprosy, syphilis, granuloma or yaws.

On 16 May 1945 Gertie left Beagle Bay and joined her siblings in Derby. Within one year Mum had followed, relieved to be with her family. The convent rules were unreasonable and her close-knit family had all left. The women who had joined the convent were considered models of Christian womanhood to their peers, yet Mum was adamant she no longer wanted to live the life of a nun. By leaving the convent she distanced herself from her superiors and abandoned the bishop's vision to have Aboriginal nuns evangelise their own.

Her reason for leaving was not totally clear, though Aggie suggested she left because the convent was not very strong. She reflected on that time, 'Katie joined the convent of her own choice and there was no pressure from our parents.' Yet Mum's leaving the convent meant there were consequences for Grampa. It meant he couldn't refer to someone in his family as having status that might benefit him in the eyes of the authorities should he need to build a case, such as when he applied for exemptions for the family. As a nun, my mother held a perceived importance in the minds of her countrimin. In his application for an exemption, Grampa's claim to having a daughter in the convent at Beagle Bay was unquestionably a bid to strengthen his chances.

Relieved to be with her family once again, Mum began work as a cook at the Club Hotel. The Fraser sisters were happy together in Derby. She soon found a second job as a nanny and home help to Harold Rowell, a Royal Flying Doctor Service pilot, and his wife, Sylvia, but it was short-lived. After one year the pilot left town and Grampa found work for Mum as a cook at Liveringa. It is where she came to know the personable young Spaniard, my father, Francisco Rodriguez.

CHAPTER 3

Leaving Galicia

He set out on a journey of a
lifetime with the Benedictines

My father was Spanish. He came from the northwest of Spain, from the province of Lugo in Galicia. The youngest of seven children, he was delivered by a midwife on the 7th of February 1921 to Maria Casanova and Jose Rodriguez in his village, Freixo.

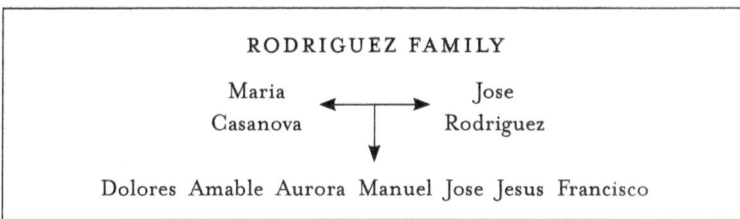

RODRIGUEZ FAMILY

Maria
Casanova ←——→ Jose
Rodriguez

Dolores Amable Aurora Manuel Jose Jesus Francisco

The northwest of Spain is extremely different to the northwest of Australia. Unlike the warm to hot climate of the Kimberley, inland Galicia experiences snows in winter and has mild summers. The region is often referred to as verde Espana (green Spain), alluding to the region's rich, fertile countryside. Bordering the Atlantic Ocean, the province is full of contrasts with a rugged coastline, rivers, endless green mountains, vineyards and pastures. Surprisingly, Galicia has a Celtic culture, which is reflected in the region's art, music and festivals. It wasn't until years later that it dawned on me why family in Galicia had sent us kids a small set of bagpipes!

The Camino de Santiago (Way of St James), an 800-kilometre pilgrimage from France, weaves its final 100 kilometres through Galicia to the medieval city of Santiago and its famous cathedral, Catedral de Santiago de Compostela. St James is the apostle believed to be buried under the cathedral. Coming from this part of the world it is little wonder then that my Dad's religious belief system was entrenched in Catholicism.

In 2010 a friend and I walked part of that final stretch starting at Samos, a Benedictine monastery, not far from Freixo. It is where Dad spent three years after being sent there as a thirteen-year-old, before coming to Australia. My reason for walking the Camino had nothing to do with religion, but was because I wanted to tread in the soil of my Galician heritage. I had grown up in the bush in the West Kimberley on Nigena country and now I had trekked in Galicia. I was a little emotional walking under huge, shady castaña (chestnut) trees, a word I was familiar with since Dad often mentioned eating them. There were plenty of symbols to remind me of him, such as when we walked behind cows being shepherded through villages. He was a child shepherd and would have done the same. But it was walking through feral eucalyptus trees from Australia that brought nostalgia as I laughed and hummed the John Williamson song 'Home Among the Gum Trees'.

Freixo is set among picturesque mountains 10 kilometres from the town of Monforte de Lemos in southern Galicia – a strikingly different landscape to the low scrub on flat, red pindan 100 kilometres east of Derby where Dad would one day build his family home. The layout of Freixo is typical of Spanish peasant villages. Interconnected buildings made from local earthen materials are surrounded with narrow, stone-edged pathways that halt fields of produce from impinging on the dwellings.

The Rodriguez family's section of the village was a two-tiered, stone-layered building with the living and sleeping areas spread across the first level, over the barn. Odours from the farm animals seeped through the wooden floors to mingle with aromas of homemade tortillas de pataca (potato omelette), salchicha (sausage), stewed polbo (octopus) and roasted castañas – a pleasant distraction from the cold nights of inland Galicia. As a toddler, Dad's mother taught him to plant vegetable seeds. Dressed in baggy dungarees with a heavy overcoat and beret, he clung closely to her. Every few paces he squatted to dig a shallow hole and carefully place a seed, before patting down the damp soil with his little hands. It is where he learned to have a keen interest in nature and in gardening.

Living a peasant's lifestyle, Dad's schooling was limited. Galego (Galician) literary tradition, along with its people, had been suppressed and ridiculed for centuries. However, since the second half of the twentieth century and with thanks to the influence of European Romanticism and the rise of provincial awareness, there has been a revival of Galician political and cultural movements. Unfortunately, a little too late for Dad.

Frank at Freixo,
September 2010
© *Cindy Solonec,*
photographer

Each day Abuela (grandmother), with her small sons in tow, herded cows into the nearby fields, to a debesa (small field) where cork, holm oaks and grass grew among the trees, providing feed for the villagers' stock. This particular debesa near Freixo was a small, one-square-acre forest – a favourite place of my Dad's. On warm days he would nap under the sun, lying on the grass while the cows and sheep fed, before shepherding them home again. A large cement trough along the way provided water for the animals, and it is where my abuela washed their clothes. In the barn, she milked the cows then made cream and cheese, taking some to sell in Monforte de Lemos.

Taking pride of place in the centre of the village stood a tiny chapel, Santa Barbara, with wooden pews and symbols of Jesus, Mary and Joseph, candles nestled at their feet. The chapel was held in great reverence by the villagers. The family regularly prayed there together. On special occasions they went to a bigger church, Santa Lucia, in nearby Guntin village. With his brothers Pepe and Jesus, the young Francisco loved to scamper around gathering empty cones and rocket tails from fireworks that lit up the evening sky on feast days and special occasions.

My father was a mischievous lad and he liked to play with fire. He first used explosives when he was about six. Stealing dynamite from Jesús, who was in charge of the town's explosives depot, he placed it under a rock, put a match to it and scurried up the hill. The blast shattered the rocks and the young muchacho (boy), along with anyone else nearby, was lucky to have not been injured. He never went near the explosives depot again. But the idea of experimenting with fire stayed with him into adult life, undertaking necessary burn-offs on his small sheep station near Derby.

As a little boy Dad often stayed with his eldest sister Dolores and her husband, Arturo Vazquez, at their village, Norcedas, 10 kilometres from Freixo. In the early morning cold, he shepherded sheep and cattle to a nearby debesa before snoozing on the soft grass where, on one such occasion, he woke to find the animals gone. Panicked, he prayed desperately to St Anthony, the patron saint of finding things, because he knew he was in big trouble. No tea until they were found.

My umbuela (grandfather), suffered a stroke when Dad was just ten years old and he lost the ability to work. Succumbing to his illness he soon moved on to the next life, leaving Abuela to care for their brood and run the small farm. As unrest in Europe intensified during the 1920s, Dad's teenage brothers Manuel, Pepe and Jesus were sent away to join the armed services, leaving their sister Amable to help Abuela run the farm. Pepe ended up in the Spanish Navy and somehow went to Russia for about forty years where he was brainwashed into being a communist. After a short stint back in Spain, he chose to move to Argentina where Manuel was living. Neither ever returned to Galicia.

Spain was on the cusp of a civil war by the early 1930s when Abuela, reluctant to have her youngest educated in a republican state education system, found another way to have him educated. As he approached the age of thirteen, she arranged for Dad to go to the Benedictine monastery at Samos, 100 kilometres away. What illusions, if any, he had about being in a monastery I can only speculate. But what I do know is that when he was told by the seminarians that it was too late for him to become a priest, he was disappointed and confused. Not scholarly enough, they said, for the priesthood. His options were to either become a labourer or return to Freixo. He chose to stay at Samos. In 1935 my dad became Brother Beda.

In 1936 the Abbot of New Norcia in Western Australia, Anslem Catalan, visited Samos. Each year the incumbent abbot travelled to Spain to entice young people to join the Benedictines abroad. Dad was so taken by Catalan's account of life in Australia and the exciting prospects for young men, it would seem, that he asked to go with them. With a civil war on the verge of engulfing Spain, Abuela was keen that he be removed from potentially brutal conflicts. Mindful of her older sons' fate, she did not want to lose her youngest to any hostilities. With a heavy heart she consented and, as an excited sixteen-year-old, Dad left Spain as the country descended into civil war.

He set out on a journey of a lifetime with the Benedictines, bound for their only monastic village in Australia. After spending several months at their monastery at Subiaco in Italy en route to Australia, Dad sailed on the *Viminale* from Genoa to Western Australia. He travelled with Abbot Catalan and several monks, arriving in Fremantle on 17 August 1937.

Migrants to Australia were required to pay a £40 landing permit and have work guaranteed. In Dad's case, the Benedictines sponsored him. There was no requirement for the missionaries to speak English, but they did have to pass a medical. His height and chest dimensions taken, eyesight and hearing tested, and other basic medical and physical details checked, he was approved for entry into Australia. The day after disembarking at Fremantle the party of Benedictines left for New Norcia. He travelled with Brother Santiago in the stores truck, a 1930s Maple Leaf, arriving at 11.45 am precisely. Just in time for lunch.

Unlike the secrecy surrounding my mother's daily activities in the 'black convent', my father's existence was well defined. As a novice monk he lived an austere life embracing the strict disciplinary 'Rule' of St Benedict. Silence, obedience and humility swaddled his days of intense labour and prayer. Prayer is considered a monk's most important work.

Dad woke early each day, even before breakfast, to join in prayers with the monks. His daily schedule of holy exercises was listed as: 9.30–10.15 focused conversations; 11.35 spiritual readings; lunch and rest; 3.45–4.30 focused conversations;

4.30–5 cell; 5–6 quiet recreation; 6–6.30 cell; 6.30–7 dinner; and 7.30 conversation and rosary. Whenever he was away from the monastery, usually working in the field, he paused to pray. In between this busy life of prayer, he tended grape vines and olive trees, worked closely with Brother Paulino in the bakery, and learned masonry.

As with most of his contemporaries, the rosy picture that Abbot Catalan had painted in his mind began to fade. Once the reality of evangelistic life set in, he contemplated the consequences of a lifetime in a monastery where few recruits remained. Knowing that he could never become a priest, my father decided not to take his final vows to become a monk. So, at twenty-one years of age, he asked for dispensation from monastic life.

On 15 July 1941 Abbot Catalan handed him an official letter stating that his request had been granted. The Apostolic Delegate, who held special faculties from the Holy See, had seen fit to excuse Dad from his vows and other religious duties. The Delegate's letter upheld that he was no longer privileged as a Benedictine novitiate. Therefore, he should go and practise the life of an el mundo (ordinary) Christian. Those who chose to leave had to find their own way back to Spain – at their own expense. Dad was keen to experience life in Australia beyond the monastery before returning to Galicia, so he chose to stay awhile. Filled with enthusiasm at the prospect of new adventures, he wasted no time and he left the monastery the very next day.

Rdo.Hno.Beda (Francisco) Rodriguez:

           Sirve el presente documento
para comunicarle,que su petición de dispensa de votos y demás
obligaciones regulares ha sido benignamente acogida por el
Sr.Delegado Apostólico,quien usando de las facultades especia-
les que la Sta.Sede le tiene concedidas,ha tenido a bien otorgar-
le cuanto usted solicitaba. Queda usted,pues,desligado de los
votos y demás deberes que tenia V.como religioso,quedando obli-
gado en el mundo a observar los deberes comunes a los demás
cristianos.

      Dios le bendiga y le tenga siempre de su mano.

                     A. Catalan, e.S.b.

        New Norcia,W.A.
        15 de Julio de 1941.

Letter of dispensation from Abbot Catalan OSB, 1941

Dad adapted well to the climate, the environment and the sparse population. Entering the world of ordinary citizens, he found work in the Upper Swan Valley, a wine-growing region near Perth. He had matured into a handsome young man. Sporting a tapered moustache, he was tall at 182 centimetres and weighing 76 kilograms. Each Sunday he went to mass at St Michaels Church on Great Eastern Highway in Midland Junction and occasionally he cycled the 50 kilometres to Scarborough Beach for a swim, staying the night in a hostel in Northbridge on his return.

A year passed before he headed further south into farming regions where he worked on wheat and dairy farms near Lake Grace and at a dehydrated-apple factory in Donnybrook. There he found the accommodation basic, even for someone who had lived an austere life for seven years. The bed was made of hessian bags and hay and he lived in the garage. Even the owner's two dogs, he quipped, had a much better deal. They had a double bed with an innerspring mattress and a big living room. Dad made friends in Donnybrook and, as luck would have it, with the Millard family. He was delighted when they found him work with their relatives on Kimberley cattle stations owned by the Emanuel Brothers.

Three years to the day after leaving New Norcia, on 15 July 1944, Dad flew to the Kimberley on an Avro Anson aircraft. He was deliberately seated beside the wheel housing where it was the passenger's job to wind up and lower the wheels with a winch. Being a strapping young fulla he seemed perfect for the job. However, his English wasn't great, and it took a while for the pilot to explain the procedure to him. All was taken with good humour. Satisfied that his pre-flight check was in order, the pilot made his way to Port Hedland, where they overnighted before continuing on to Broome, Derby and finally to Fitzroy Crossing.

The Emanuel Brothers' cattle empire in the central and west Kimberley was made up of several stations that included Cherabun, Christmas Creek and Gogo. All were run by Ted Millard, who immediately sent Dad to Christmas Creek where his nephew, Vic Jones, was the manager. It was at this time that Dad started to keep a diary. Like the Benedictine monks, he would keep an account of his movements – to some extent at least. For the next six years he wrote in Spanish. A few words here, a sentence there, but rarely anything longer. Given his teenage disappointment at not being academic enough to become a priest, my father was determined to educate himself. The fact that he even kept a diary is remarkable and it is no surprise then that he became literate in and a fluent speaker of English. He enjoyed reading about world events and Spanish history. As his time in the West Kimberley grew into years, he captured snippets of his life, the catalyst for me in deciding to write our family's story.

Dad's very first job involved formwork. At Blood Wood stock camp he cemented a tank and there he met the camp manager, John Marshall, and his new bride, Nita. The three became good friends and Dad enjoyed moving around with the Marshall's' camp. At Dusty Camp he learned to brand and geld cattle – and this is where he learned to ride. His new mates didn't mind taking the micky out of him, a 'clean skin' who spoke a strange version of English. They encouraged him to hop on a mule that then threw him, to their chortles. He got along well with the Aboriginal fullas and together they clowned around making fun of Vic Jones, until they realised he was a crack shot who always carried a revolver. They became a little wary of the boss and his readiness to use his gun.

To the young shepherd turned novice monk, turned mason, station work was intense and it was tiring. Mustering, branding and drafting, they slowly moved cattle from one site to the next, edging closer to the Gogo homestead. From there, during the dry months, cattle were herded by droving contractors 500 kilometres to the Broome meatworks.

*Frank, having
learned to
ride a horse.
Source unknown*

Vic Jones was impressed with Dad's masonry skills and by the
end of August he raised his pay from £3 to £4 a week. Dad realised, though, that he needed official qualifications in building
and masonry to ensure work came his way into the future. So he
enrolled in correspondence courses with Stott's College in Perth
and the International Correspondence Schools. He worked late
into the night to complete assignments, keen to the hilt to gain
accreditation. Again, this was quite a feat considering his imperfect English, the improbability of qualified tutors and the time it
must have taken for assignments to be returned.

Dad was attracted to new work opportunities and in 1945
he headed to the Yampi Sound, north of Derby. The war had
ended and development had recommenced at the iron ore mines
on Cockatoo and Koolan Islands operated by Broken Hill Pty
Ltd (now BHP). But the pay was no better than on the station,
while union strikes meant days off work without pay. While on

the island, Ted Millard wrote to him saying his job was always there if he wanted it. Dad decided to return to station work.

At Christmas Creek he laid the foundations for the first house he would build in the Kimberley. It was Tuesday, 23 October 1945 when he arrived at the site with Ted Millard and Vic Jones. Together they measured the ground from where the manager's house would materialise. Then Millard and Jones left, leaving Dad as the sole architect and builder. He set about manually churning cement in drums and moulding bricks with his bare hands from local sands and stones. This building, he was certain, could never be destroyed.

Dad made the most of any leisure time gardening, reading and writing. Raised in farmland Galicia where his keen interest in nature evolved, his fascination now shifted to the Kimberley bush, leading him to experiment. He tried grafting introduced figs onto wild fruit but soon realised that grafting a deciduous tree onto a native tree was just not going to work. He would learn from his mistakes and he had success in gardening wherever he lived in the region. My dad was a good correspondent, keeping in regular contact with his family in Spain, his brothers in South America, the Millards down south and the monks at New Norcia. And he regularly received the Catholic paper, *The Record*.

Once he completed the building at Christmas Creek, and with no impending construction at the time, Dad left the Emanuel Brothers in May 1946 to return to Cockatoo Island. His reputation as a hard-working, capable and reliable builder was gaining traction in the region – he could pick and choose his work. As always, he made it his business to meet any local

Catholic priests during his ventures and he paid a visit to Father Albert Scherzinger in Derby before heading offshore. Over a cuppa the priest asked him to build a church. Derby had become a parish that year and it was only fitting that it should have a church. In the interim, mass and holy devotions were held in the sisters' cottage or, on significant holy days like Good Friday, in the Roads Board Hall. Dad agreed, but no commencement date was set.

While still in Derby, as he sat on the verandah of the Club Hotel contemplating jotting in his diary, he watched as a tall, refined-looking gudia man dressed in stockman's khakis and bush hat approached him. The man introduced himself as Kim Rose, the manager of Liveringa Station. He had heard about Frank Rodriguez and now he offered him work with the Kimberley Pastoral Company at Liveringa.

Rose then left and while Dad thought over the offer, a house-maid came out onto the verandah. The young woman introduced herself as Katie Fraser. As the two chatted he mentioned that he had been offered work at Liveringa, and in turn she disclosed that her dad, who was an overseer at Liveringa, had just found her a job there. She was heading out in July. He also met her sisters, Frances and Gertie, who worked at the hotel. The three Fraser women decided that the stranger was French, and not bad looking either.

A few days later, sitting in his quarters on Cockatoo catching up on diary entries, he wrote, 'All day in Derby. Kim Rose offered me a job to work on his station, but I declined. I went to Cockatoo Island instead. Tonight I embarked on the Yampi. One of my friends was half drunk and he fell in the sea and now everything looks very cheerful on the Yampi'. Dad helped to rescue Jack Stone, who had not only borrowed money from him, but he fancied Katie. So Dad gave more thought to Liveringa and after a short stint on Cockatoo, accepted the Rose offer.

He arrived at Liveringa on 16 July 1946. He liked the look of this place, set among spinifex-covered rocky hills and close to the Mardoowarra floodplains. Based in the blacksmith's workshop, Dad became a jack of all trades – mason, mechanic and all-round handyman, but primarily the builder. Within a few days of arriving he met the station's overseer, Fred Fraser.

Grampa Fraser, Liveringa, 1946
© Kevan Rose, photographer

CHAPTER 4

Getting mixed up

Some whitefullas who wed Aboriginal women
didn't talk to their wife's parents

G rampa stood at the door to the blacksmith's workshop. He wore a huge grin as he called to Dad, 'Donde yo soy hay muchas castañas,' (where I come from there are many chestnuts). He knew how to make the newcomer feel welcome. 'Fulgentius Fraser,' he said as he shook Dad's hand, 'but everyone calls me Fred.' Dressed in customary stockman's gear – khaki shirt, sleeves rolled up, long trousers strapped under a portly girth, muddied riding boots complete with a stockman's hat – Grampa was distinguishable by a pipe dangling on his bottom lip.

He had learned to speak Spanish at Drysdale River. Now Dad felt a strong sense of belonging since he, too, had connections with the Benedictine monks. He chuckled at Grampa's vernacular, deciding that the old man's Spanish wasn't too bad. And why wouldn't it be? After all, Grampa spoke a few Australian languages. 'Ahhh, roasted castañas indeed,' Dad reminisced. He missed his mother's cooking.

Anchored higher up the hill from the workshop was the homestead. Colourful exotic flowers meticulously tended to by Kim Rose's wife, Pat, bloomed on the escarpment leading up to the house. The building faced south over the extensive Mardoowarra floodplains exhibiting lush grasses and trees that hosted an abundance of wildlife. At the bottom of the hill a large billabong sighed quietly among rich foliage, waiting for rains to quench its thirst and once again fill the floodplains. Healthy vegetable gardens thrived on its banks, providing the station people with fresh produce.

Safe from any raging flood, the homestead was being adapted to suit European family comforts. With wide verandahs, a tennis court at the back and terraced lawns at the front overlooking the floodplains, the homestead perched gallantly above its lesser buildings, signalling the hierarchal system that operated from there. At the bottom of the hill in a fenced-in compound, Aboriginal workers and their families camped.

As they chatted, Dad thought there was something familiar about Grampa's face. Fred Fraser reminded him of his new boss, Kim Rose. He then became more interested and listened keenly to what the old man was saying. His eldest daughter was coming to work at Liveringa. She'd been working in town and now she had a job here. Dad felt a sense of excitement but he simply smiled and said nothing. My mother's arrival was imminent and Grampa had come from Willumbah to meet her.

It was 27 July 1946, just eleven days after Dad had arrived at the station, when Mum made her appearance. Together with the Roses and Grampa, Dad walked down the hill as dust rose in the distance and the sound of a motor announced her arrival across the valley. Bishop Raible was giving Mum a lift on his station rounds, probably in the hope he might change Mum's mind about leaving the 'black convent'. He parked his jalopy near the shearing shed.

Dad watched as Mum hopped down from the passenger seat. She was a fine-looking woman. Sensibly dressed in a knee-length dress and lightweight cardigan to ward off the cool July breeze, her hair neatly pinned back in a bun matched the colour of her dark brown eyes. She carried herself with stately poise. A no-nonsense exterior belied my mother's warm and considerate nature, ensuring that potential young suitors shied away from any chivalrous ideas.

She embraced her father and politely nodded to the boss and his wife as she was introduced. Dad stepped forward and Grampa introduced them, 'This is Frank Rodriguez, the builder.' 'I know,' she acknowledged to her father. 'We met in Derby.' Dad picked up her suitcase and showed her to her room. 'We thought you were French,' she laughed. They knew they would get along. Mum's room was adjacent to the perishable store and the workers' kitchen – she liked it immediately. It looked comfortable with a splendid view of the billabong and the floodplains.

My parents' mutual attraction was instantaneous and by the end of that year, they were married. The speed at which they became engaged and set a wedding date probably had something to do with her determination not to return to the convent. A wedding was the best way to stave off unwanted pressure. She confided in Dad, telling him that both Bishop Raible and Grampa wanted her to return to the convent. But there was no family at Beagle Bay now. They were all gone, and she missed them. When she asked Dad to marry her, he understood. Taken a little off guard, he nonetheless accepted.

Katie and Frank, Derby, 1940s. Source unknown

Wanting to be sure that the young couple's decision was sincere, the Bishop returned to Liveringa in August. Mum remained steadfast and Dad backed her. He had a fair idea what it meant to dedicate your life to God as a subservient member of an abbey. Abbot Catalan's sage advice to live as an ordinary Christian resonated in him now and he supported Mum to do the same. Satisfied with their decision, Bishop Raible agreed to marry them on 8 December that year, the day of the Feast of the Immaculate Conception. He then listened to confessions, said mass and continued on his station rounds. Now Dad would have to build the church in Derby.

Liveringa was an incessant hive of activity with much movement in and out of the homestead surrounds – and with little wonder. The main road connecting Derby and Fitzroy Crossing and the stations in between ran close to the river. Dad's first job was to build the shearers' quarters and to complete the homestead kitchen, from where he watched the comings and goings of travellers. In his diary he noted trucking agents Harry Sadler and Joe Smith pass through with a load of cargo for stations further east while Don Sears, an overseer at nearby Lulugui Station, arrived with his pack horses. Together with Grampa, he called on Dad to introduce himself and to see how the shearers' quarters were coming along.

As it neared shearing time in the middle of August, workers from neighbouring stations began arriving to help. Extended family from Mount Anderson Station, Bluegum and William Watson came to prepare the yards and the shearing shed while Canny Rose, Kim's cousin who ran Mount Anderson 32 kilometres away towards Derby, was a regular visitor.

At least once a fortnight a mail plane landed and Dad would wait expectantly. More often than not he had mail. Sometimes from the Trevanians, who he'd befriended at Lake Grace, his sister Dolores in Galicia, brother Manuel in Argentina, stamps from Mr Crane the Derby postmaster, a package with his latest assignments and, on one occasion, a letter from Fossil Downs Station offering him work.

Dad travelled to Derby in September to build the church, while Mum stayed at Liveringa. He had promised her he would first call on her mother and her siblings. Granny was a petite woman, he noticed, darker than her daughters with obvious

Indian features accentuated by high cheekbones. Like my Mum, her hair was neatly tied back in a bun. Granny was very much the Fraser matriarch.

As Dad sat with her at the kitchen table chatting, they were interrupted only briefly by the younger ones, Dottie, Jimmy and Leena, running in to meet him. Frances, Edna and Gertie sat quietly nearby nattering and glancing sideways at their older sister's Don Juan. They deliberated over whether he would be good enough for her. But, really, they knew better than to worry because Gertie had seen a picture of the Blessed Mary near his suitcase when she cleaned his hotel room. Having a shared religion meant that they had a shared worldview. Like Aboriginal cultures, European peasant societies have a strong sense of kin and both my parents came from supportive families. Fortunately for Dad, my mother had a wide network of relatives that had evolved out of the displacement of Kimberley kids to Beagle Bay and Drysdale River.

Development in the Kimberley slowly picked up post-WWII, but finances and building materials were scant. The Pallottine missionaries needed divine intervention if the Spanish carpenter was to build their church. Dad found timber in the most obscure places, salvaging pieces from the jetty that had fallen into the sea and had come back in with the tides. People who lived alongside the marsh in Derby (where the caravan park is now) built their own homes from scrounged materials. Known colloquially as 'Indian Territory', one couple who lived there built their floor from wooden shipping pallets then partially covered it with linoleum. The bulk of the materials for the church came from a disused air force base at Noonkanbah Station, 250 kilometres east of Derby. Abandoned after the war, there was a runway, hangars and army barracks still in good nick that were a welcome source of building materials for people in the region. The base proved to be the Pallottines' godsend. Galvanised iron huts were dismantled and transported to Derby for the Catholic church.

On the 25th of September Dad began laying the foundations. With the help of ex-Beagle Bay and Lombadina menfolk – Ambrose Cox, Albert Kelly, Tom Puertollano and Jerome Manado – he assembled the church. He made cement blocks 4 feet high and placed them around the perimeter to raise the frame. With improvisation being a Derby trademark, the men layered the floor with bitumen. Dad would have to cement the floor at a later date, when supplies were available and he could find the time to complete any additions. For now, though, a bitumen floor would have to do.

Paint was in short supply too, so he agreed to pay a painter, Campbell Dempster, two guineas for a small amount even though Dempster was selling army surplus. A shrewd character, he even had a cool drink factory at Noonkanbah where he made drinks with muddy water from the billabong, disguising the taste with plenty of sugar. Dad purchased a couple of bottles. They tasted okay he decided – and countrimin too seemed to like it.

The church steadily progressed. As Dad sat one afternoon enjoying a cuppa after having said the rosary with Father Albert, he was grateful for the light breeze that cooled his body. Watching the priest, he wondered how he ever managed in the long, priestly garb that clung to his sweaty body. Dad realised that he may well have dodged a bullet as far as dressing appropriately for the Kimberley climate went.

'What should we call the church Frank?' Fr Albert asked. 'How about "The Holy Rosary", the same as the main church near Freixo in Lugo,' Dad suggested. Fr Albert smiled and nodded. He liked it. It was the least that he could do given the financial difficulties the missionaries faced in trying to establish their missions around the Kimberley. The Holy Rosary Church is believed to be the first Catholic church to have been built in Derby.

Holy Rosary Church, Derby, 1970s © Sam Oriti, photographer

Whenever he could, Dad headed to Liveringa where he and Mum planned their wedding. As they chatted over tea with stocksmen Ernie Carvolth and Barney Lawford, they became more and more aware of how marginalised peoples were controlled by gudia. Bigotry was not new to my Dad. As a non-English speaking migrant he had copped his fair share of prejudice. During the war, while still down south, someone dobbed him in to the authorities saying he was a spy. And at another time, while taking photos with his box camera in Perth, the police asked him what he was doing. They then suggested he might be better off going north. Perhaps that's why the Donnybrook Millards offered him work with their relatives. He had even wanted to join the Australians who were hell bent on fighting for 'their country' but he was denied the chance because, as a migrant, he didn't qualify. New to the Kimberley, Dad had to report to the police station at Fitzroy Crossing and inform the authorities of his whereabouts.

He and my mother's interracial union was not without the opinions and attitudes of others in 1940s Australia. Some reckoned white and black people shouldn't marry. Dad had always moved comfortably between cultures but now some were not impressed with his choice of girlfriend. The Millards at Gogo were a case in point. They opposed the marriage. On a visit to Derby for the annual horse-racing round, they paid him a visit to see how the church was coming along and to have a chat about his relationship. They made it quite clear they were not happy. Dad chose to ignore them and his diary entry demonstrates how uneasy this conversation made him, 'Making small preparations to start work on the church and it's the last day of the races. Had a small conversation with Arthur Millard and his wife. They were not pleased with the idea about my oncoming marriage. God have mercy on me'.

Dad was well aware of disparaging attitudes towards Aboriginal people and the Millard's' words were an uncomfortable reminder. When Mum heard about their visit, doubt set in. She wondered if it was a mistake to be marrying a white man. She probed him, concerned that some gudia men who marry Aboriginal women stay away from their wife's parents. She was worried that, once again, like her time in the convent, she would see less of her family.

But she needn't worry, he reassured her. Everything would be fine. After all, he and her father were good mates.

Nonetheless, ostracism towards them increased. Tony Ozies, who was working at Liveringa at the time, put things into perspective when I interviewed him at his home at Banana Well, north of Broome, in 2003, 'The whitefullas had no respect for Aboriginal people. When the war was over, the whites couldn't cohabitate. It was okay by Neville for Frank and Katie, but Frank then wasn't allowed to go up to the top house if he married Katie. He wasn't allowed up there for a cup of tea.'

My parents were to be married without any government interference, even though neither was an Australian citizen. It was more meaningful to them anyway to have the church's approval and blessing than that of the state. With Bishop Raible set to consecrate their marriage, they asked Gertie Fraser and Tom Puertollano to be their attendants.

Their wedding day came with glitches, even if self-inflicted. Grampa didn't make it to their big event. Two days before, he had taken Dad fishing at Cuttings on the banks of the Mardoowarra near the Yeeda homestead and it was probably the cold lamb they ate that gave them both food poisoning. Grampa was the worse off given Dad did go to the doctor. Grampa was so sick that Tom's brother, Alphonse Puertollano, gave Mum away. As she walked down the aisle of the Holy Rosary Church, her shoe became stuck in the bitumen floor and Alphonse couldn't yank it out. She married her Spanish builder wearing just one shoe. Following the ceremony they visited Grampa, who managed to sit up and embrace them warmly. The wedding breakfast was held at Aggie and Tom's place with the Bishop in attendance.

The guests partied into the night, singing and dancing. Dad didn't go. He was so darn sick he lay alongside Grampa on the verandah, watching his wedding celebrations from afar.

Tom, Frank, Katie and Gertie, Derby, 1946. Source unknown

Mum and Dad settled into married life on Liveringa. They set up home in a worker's cottage that Dad had built on a hill lower down from the homestead and they furnished it with much of his handiwork. They busied themselves in their respective jobs and made good use of their spare time. Allowed to use the tennis court up at the top house, they enjoyed the odd game or they played cards at home in the evenings. But mostly my parents explored the surrounding terrain. They often visited Grampa at Willumbah and picnicked by the billabong, where they fished and set jarramba (freshwater prawns) traps and Dad occasionally shot a crocodile.

He eventually bought his first vehicle. It was a Chevrolet ute, ex Lulugui, that Dad paid the KPC £60 for. Despite needing a lot of repairs, they could now venture away from the homestead. They took trips to town to see the family, to go to mass and they regularly went to the outdoor pictures – almost as often as they went to church. Great old movies in those days like *The Spanish Man* (1945) and *Madonna of the Seven Moons* (1945). Occasionally one of the station workers would go with them. Pat Rose told Dad that her husband was concerned about selling him the truck because he thought he might never see Dad again.

It also meant that their ventures into the bush were often beset with problems. An axle would break, flat tyres were regular, they got bogged or they lost their way. Dad spent a lot of time with his head under the bonnet. It's how he learned about mechanics – bush mechanics. He pulled the motor to pieces then put it together again many times. The car proved to be popular with others too. Tom sometimes borrowed it, as did Kim Rose, who paid Dad a few quid for petrol. Dad reckoned Rose preferred it to go bush in because he was precious about his own nice vehicle.

In January 1947 Dad rushed Mum to the Derby hospital with suspected appendicitis. There never was a clear diagnosis of her condition, yet her appendix was removed anyway. This would be the first of many visits and admissions to hospitals that would afflict my mother throughout her life.

My parents' togetherness was becoming stronger. They were a well-connected couple and their shared Christian values ensured they cared for one another and their extended families. Their devotion to Catholicism played a significant part in safeguarding a commitment to one another. To understand this bond is to understand Catholic traditions. Both embraced values that are inscribed in seven sacraments (rites) that manifested in their actions – Baptism, Confirmation, Eucharist, Penance, Anointing of the Sick, Marriage and Holy Orders. The whole liturgical life of the Church revolves around the Eucharistic sacrifice and the sacraments. The sacraments were my parents' code of ethics that guided the way they lived their lives. They knew that if the teachings of the Church were obeyed and practised in this life, they were ensured of an idyllic existence in the next.

The sacraments became our family's rites of passage. Each of us kids was given a Christian name, found suitable godparents and baptised within weeks of our birth, and sent to Catholic schools. Mass on Sundays and on Holy Days of Obligation was compulsory. It didn't matter that we lived on stations because a visiting priest often said mass in our homes, while the rosary and other meditative prayers were recited whenever and wherever practicable. If we were in transit somewhere – out in the bush – we said the rosary together as we drove along.

In all likelihood, my father had no reason to question his worldview and the power of prayer. His upbringing had made sure of that. Mum, on the other hand, had her doubts. She was a first-generation mission-born woman and, while heavily influenced by Catholicism, she had nonetheless listened to the 'old people' who lived on the outskirts of the mission, and their inherent beliefs. She questioned the supposed power of prayer that did not prevent the illnesses that plagued her life. Even though she prayed to God, her ailments never really improved. When in her poorest moments, she would ask Dad, 'Where is this God of ours?'

Dad continued with the Liveringa building program, only interrupting it as shearing time approached to help around the sheep runs. It took a shearing team up to five weeks to complete the job on the massive Liveringa lease before moving on to the next station. Grampa often had a meal with the young couple as he edged his flock closer to the homestead, updating them on the trials and tribulations of the station. A serious problem was presenting in the region. Some sheep had died, he told them, lost to the curse of corkscrew grass that twisted its way through the sheep's wool into the body, and sometimes into the heart. The damaging effect of corkscrew was one of many complications that beset the local sheep industry.

———

Shearing done, Mum and Dad prepared for a long overdue honeymoon. She was keen to show him where she was born and where she had grown up. At the invitation of Bishop Raible they headed to Beagle Bay and with them went a cheerful young Edna. They stopped over for a night in Broome where Mum introduced her new husband to family and friends. He was delighted to find himself warmly welcomed by her extended family, in particular by Aunty Grace and Uncle Vincent Martin. The Martins had been at Drysdale River with Granny and Grampa and they remained long-time close friends of the family.

The next morning the trio headed to Beagle Bay with the Bishop. He proudly showed Dad around the mission, especially the church. Of course, Dad closely inspected the workmanship and took in all aspects of the church's carpentry. He claimed it looked first class. He noted not only the quality of the bush timber used, but also the way it all had been fitted skilfully together and he was captivated by the amount of shells embedded in the altar. Not to be outdone Brother Matthias, who had offered a Dad a bed for his stay, showed off *his* blacksmith shop and the mission's gardens. The vegetable garden was his pride and joy. Dad was in awe.

The two women stayed in the black convent and together the three of them went to mass and benediction several times during their short stay. Dad visited the sisters and he joined in a football match before they headed off with the Aboriginal nuns to go camping at Midligon, a favourite childhood spot by the beach. It is where the Fraser siblings often went with Nygumi, a place that held special memories for Mum and Edna. After a few days of eating, laughing, singing and reminiscing along with fishing and just relaxing, the group returned to the mission. Mum's good friend Clare 'Malley' Sibasado took her vows as a nun on 24 May. Satisfied with having been there for Malley's special moment and at having had a honeymoon to remember, Mum and Dad headed home to Liveringa.

When Mum fell pregnant not long after her appendectomy, she felt the need to be closer to her family, so they left the station and moved to Derby. Perhaps the visit to her childhood home had rekindled an uneasy feeling of being around gudia, bearing in mind Tony Ozies' and the Millards' comments. She wondered whether she would be better off having her babies delivered by Aboriginal midwives like her mother had – but it was white nurses who delivered babies now. They moved to Derby at the end of August 1947 where they rented a house from the St John of God Sisters.

As they awaited the birth of their first child, Dad resumed work on the church. First he overlaid the bitumen floor with concrete then added steps up to the altar. There was no shortage of jobs around town as he busied himself with formwork, housing maintenance and work on the wharf. The State Shipping Service remained a vital link to and from the north, transporting cargo, passengers and stock. Derby was a major port from where cattle were sent to Fremantle or exported to Singapore, and wool was sent to the southern markets. Because Derby experiences one of the most extreme tidal movements in the world, ships on the Singapore route, the *Charon* and the *Gorgon*, were specifically built to handle these tides. The bases of the ships had been strengthened to allow them to settle on the mud at low tide.

Dad also worked in the general store, McGovern and Thompson, which the locals nicknamed 'money-grabs and thieves', probably because they felt they were being charged more than necessary by the owners. He served customers and distributed cases of fruit and vegetables around town whenever a cargo vessel was in, and he packaged up station orders. As a capable handyman, Dad proved to be a useful asset aside from running the store.

Catalina Dolores arrived on the 27th of December 1947 and my parents were overjoyed. But she survived for only four days. There was no explanation for the baby's death and my shattered parents were left to speculate. She was supposedly born healthy.

December was hot and the hospital did not have cribs – just prams that were covered with mosquito nets. I wonder if this contributed to my sister's death. Grief stricken, my parents were comforted by two gudia women who told Dad that they had baptised the baby. His diary entry evokes a depth of devotion from which he drew solace. Living far from his family and the empathy of his mother and his siblings, especially his sisters, he wept,

> *Today had the very sad news of the death of my infant daughter Catalina Dolores. Great sadness because God is the Honour of everything and our love belongs to Him. She will be an Angel close to God looking into the face of God, our Creator. Something is not quite right that she only lived for four days in this world. She was born on the 27th of December at night and God took her away on the 31st of the same month.*

My parents buried their baby in the old Derby cemetery.

———

Together with strength and the benefit of prayer, Mum and Dad got on with their lives and they decided to buy a block of land before returning to Liveringa. First, though, they had to deal with an administrative hurdle. Neither was an Australian citizen. To be eligible to purchase land they had to be naturalised so it was imperative that they apply. Dad was the first to submit an application and on the 17th of April 1948 he became an Australian citizen.

Mum had to apply under the *Natives (Citizenship Rights) Act*. At first she had ignored the offer of citizenship. It was ludicrous to her that a piece of paper could change someone from being an Aboriginal to being a gudia, of sorts. Her sister Frances, too, observed a self-imposed boycott, declaring, 'I never applied for citizenship – didn't apply for it, didn't believe I needed it'. Reminiscent of when she was a novitiate and had applied for an exemption from the *Aborigines Act 1905*, where Mum was also expected to deny her Aboriginality, she once again faced controlling laws based on Western ideologies. The declaration on her citizenship application stated, 'For the two years prior to the date hereof I have dissolved native and tribal association except with respect to lineal descendants or native relations of the first degree.' She signed the form for a fee of 10 shillings, agreeing on paper to abandon her inherent customs and live as westerners do. If her application to become an Australian citizen was successful, she would be entitled to limited rights. It was approved on the 23rd of September 1948.

Eventually, my parents bought the block and Mum went on to break every rule. My defiant mother spoke her Aboriginal languages and, with Dad and her whole extended family, she indulged in bush culinary delights to her heart's content.

Following the loss of their firstborn, my parents returned to Liveringa and continued life as they had left it. He, busy on buildings while she worked in the lower kitchen. About fifty people, mostly blackfullas, lived around the station. Propping up Kimberley pastoral interests was an underpaid, if paid at all, black workforce. Many people were in our extended families. While 'mixed-descent' and gudia workers received cash wages, our countrimin were paid with flour, sugar and tea.

They helped build the station's infrastructure – stockyards, fences, windmills, tanks, troughs – and the women, generally whose last names we never knew or whether they even had one, worked as domestics in the top house. Each person was known by their first name, while gudias were called 'mister' or 'missus'. As for the 'mixed-descent' people, they tended to be 'aunty' or 'uncle'.

Pat Rose was good to bush people, recalled my cousin Patsy 'Ginya' Yambo. Patsy did house cleaning with other 'full-descent' family like Aunty Maggie and Aunty Wabbi, while Fanny, Kitty, Nancy and Daisy all helped to look after the boss's kids. Topsy was the boss in the lower kitchen, where she baked the station's bread, cut it up and handed it to the camp mob as they lined up at the kitchen window.

When Pat Rose's younger daughter June and her husband, Henry Gooch, moved to Blina Station 80 kilometres away in the early 1960s, some of the Liveringa mob went with them. June asked if anyone wanted to go. She didn't think for one minute that they would because they lived next to the lovely billabong at Liveringa. But, 'the dear old things Maggie and Molly and Bewie and Fanny and Mary came with us over to Blina, which I thought was fantastic. I would never have managed without them looking after our babies in the stock camp when I helped Henry.'

Audrey, June's older sister, often sat with my Mum, listening to her stories about Beagle Bay. How she went fishing from the beach and smashed oysters off the rocks while keeping an eye open for octopus tentacles so they didn't latch on to her legs. Dottie, Jimmy and Leena spent school holiday time between Liveringa with Mum and at Willumbah with Granny and Grampa where, together with the station kids, they explored the hilly terrain and swam in floodways and creeks during rain time. Sitting by the billabong, the kids watched the men cut and pound mangroves, then spread them over the water so the fish couldn't breathe, cheering as they skilfully speared the fish coming up to the surface.

Grampa, with Jimmy, June and Leena on Moogali, Liveringa, 1950s.
Source unknown

Station hands found novel ways of boosting their income by culling marauding dingoes and wedge-tailed eagles that preyed on the stock. The mauling of newborn lambs was a big problem so the local shire offered a generous bounty for pelts, eagle claws and beaks, enticing station workers to come up with innovative ways of trapping. Dad and Grampa had fun trying to outdo each other and Kim Rose joined in. He gave Dad a few eagles on the quiet, since Dad had a lesser chance of catching a decent swag than did Grampa, who worked out in the far reaches of the station. The most common way to snare a dingo was to smear a goat or kangaroo carcass with poison, then place it under loosened spinifex.

The rationale behind the wage disparity between black and white people was the myth that Aboriginals wouldn't survive the evils of money. Moreover, the KPC justified their not paying cash wages by claiming they did not want to upset neighbouring stations that were not as financially grounded as they. Gudia folk, on the other hand, spent the profits made through the loyalty and hard work of their Aboriginal workers to feather their own nests, while proper living conditions for the workers were left wanting. Under the rules of the Department of Native Affairs, stations were supposed to ensure there was suitable accommodation with enough food and adequate water for drinking and bathing, but little notice was taken. Managers were remiss in their duties towards workers in the camp. Perhaps this was because, according to one welfare inspector, 'full-descent' people at Liveringa who lived in spinifex huts appeared healthy and were well clothed. That 'full-descent' people should work for no wages was considered 'a given' by pastoralists.

Camped nearby on Noonkanbah Station were about one hundred people, men, women, children, the elderly and the sick, with about sixty per cent able to work. Noonkanbah is on the homelands of the 'upper' Nigena people. There are two sections to Nigena and my family are from the lower end, closer to Derby along the Mardoowarra. The station had become home to displaced Walmajarri, Mangala and Dualin/Yulbaridja people who had come in from the desert. They had been pushed off their homelands when their waterholes – which belong to families with their knowledges securely embedded in oral deposit boxes – were destroyed and wells built along the Canning Stock Route around 1904, long before Grampa's droving days.

Like at Liveringa, Noonkanbah's 'mixed-descent' employees were paid in cash while 'full-descent' workers were given some clothes and blankets in lieu. The management's logic was that 'natives' were more content without wages, free from the vices of alcohol and gambling. Station managers were possessive of their black workers, who they considered as property, and they didn't like it when workers moved to other stations. Grampa, loyal to his countrimin, found himself in a spot of bother on one occasion for giving work to men from Myroodah who had moved to Willumbah. The neighbouring managers complained to Kim Rose and Grampa was reprimanded.

———

During the 1940s, further south in the Pilbara, working and living conditions for Aboriginals were shoddy and people felt shame that they were not paid wages. Aboriginal people in the region knew damn well that it kept them inferior, while pastoralists tried to downplay the treatment by saying they were their carers, giving Aboriginals a place to live while letting them access their very own country. Various Pilbara groups banded together and took matters into their own hands to challenge the unfair practices. They organised a major strike to coincide with both the International Workers' Day on the 1st of May 1946 and the beginning of the mustering and shearing season. The strike drew a lot of support. Unions nationally and community organisations in Perth stepped up. In the port of Fremantle, unionists refused to handle wool from any northwest station that had used Aboriginal workers as cheap labour. The strike lasted until 1949, and some say even longer.

The Pilbara walk-off put government authorities in the West Kimberley on notice. It pricked the consciousness of the Native Affairs Department in Derby, which didn't want similar unrest in its neck of the woods. Acting Commissioner McBeath was convinced that what had happened in the Pilbara could be avoided if treatment of Kimberley people was met with common sense and empathy. He was adamant that a gradual improvement in their living arrangements and healthy food was doable.

In 1949 a travelling inspector visited Liveringa and reported that Kim Rose claimed to be handling the matter carefully because labour was scarce. It was a tribal custom, Rose touted, for Aboriginal people to be mobile. Therefore, he never pressured them into staying and he found it difficult to make the 'natives' stay put anyway. The inspector said he thought Rose was only saying what he needed to say, to satisfy his standing in the pastoral community. Rose, he said, was empathic and keen to improve conditions for his workers. Regardless, the KPC was told to improve conditions as soon as possible. All-weather huts, an ablution block with water connections and septic system, and cement floors with proper drainage must be installed. Forty-four-gallon drums were to be placed around the camp for rubbish and emptied regularly. The advice was well received and the KPC moved to make improvements. Together with Dad, Kim Rose began devising a building plan.

Two months after Dad began in all earnest to upgrade the Aboriginals' housing compound at Liveringa, he received notification that he had become a certified carpenter in roofing and steel square. His six years of study had paid off,

Kim Rose arrived from Perth in the evening; also his brother Canny was with him. I received a bit of mail, a letter from my sister Amable, after a long time. Katie received two visitors. The father-in-law also is here today. I also received a certificate for my studies from the ICS [International Correspondence Schools] that made me happy; also a gift from Kim Rose, a pocket-knife.

Dad installed two toilets in the compound and by mid-October he had started work on a large Nissen hut with wire tray beds fitted to the walls for everyone to share. It was expected that the Aboriginal workers, their families and all, would snooze happily together in the one building. But no-one wanted to sleep in them. Not only did bush people prefer to live outdoors, but the open-plan Nissen hut was culturally inappropriate. Relationship taboos meant women avoided eye contact with their sons-in-law, and they were never allowed to be in each other's company. Outdoor living in disposable humpies was preferred where people could continue to practise their customs. Others just slept in the shearing shed.

Dad's employment at Liveringa meant he was a significant contributor to the station's overall building program. The workers' cottages, the Nissen hut, the swimming pool and the meat house he built, and he made extensions and renovations to existing structures. He erected windmills and fences and he helped out at shearing time. Respect for his skill and work ethic did not go unnoticed by Broken Hill Proprietary's (BHP) chief general manager and friend of the Roses, Essington Lewis. Travelling by company plane, the executive sometimes retreated to Liveringa during his business trips to Yampi Sound. He liked Dad and he visited him on site, bringing tools and even oranges from South Australia. Rolling up his sleeves, Lewis seemed to enjoy getting down to manual labouring, helping out Dad.

Liveringa Station, 1950s. Source unknown

Dad's craftsmanship went beyond construction as Audrey Bullough pointed out to me. 'Some of the beautiful things I remember that Frank made, you can see how creative the Spanish are. Look at Gaudi!' She credited Dad for suggesting to her mother that terracing and gardens on the rock could be turned into something spectacular. Audrey's own father sought my Dad's advice about landscaping and buildings. 'Frank must have been brilliant and had engineering feats. He put in septic tanks before the "big shots" of Derby had such modern luxuries. The meat house was state of the art, specifically designed with dripping tray and covered with flywire. Under the meat house was the dairy.' Dad constructed a swimming pool on the terracing, where he had my sister Pepita when she was just ten months old place her little foot alongside June and Jarran Rose in the wet cement. The footprints are still there today.

Footprints of June Rose, Josephine (Pepita) and Jarran Rose next to the Liveringa swimming pool, August 1950.
© Dieter Solonec, photographer

Never far from my parents' thoughts and conversations after the loss of Dolores was the desire to try again to start a family. With faith unfaltering and in an attempt to ensure there would be no repeat misfortunes, on the 11th of March 1949 they began a novena – nine consecutive days of prayer – to St Joseph for another child. St Joseph was not only the patron saint of carpenters and of the universe, he was the husband of Mary and the foster father of Jesus. Perhaps it is why they prayed to him to ensure the safe delivery of another child.

St Joseph did listen because a healthy, bouncing daughter arrived in the Derby hospital nine months later on the 10th of November. Relieved, Dad conveyed to his diary, 'Today a daughter was born Josefa Catalina, T.G [Thank God].' This time there were no complications. They named her Josephine Kathleen after Dad's brother Pepe (Jose) in Argentina and after Mum – and, in all likelihood, after St Joseph. My older sister became known as 'Pepita', Spanish for Josephine.

Frank and Pepita, Liveringa, 1950 © Katie Rodriguez, photographer

During this time Dad and Tom were recognised for their services to the Catholic Church. On the recommendation of Bishop Raible, they were honoured with the Pro Ecclesia et Pontifice (The Church and the Pope). The two received a medal and a certificate signed and blessed by Pope Pius XII – an ultimate reward from the Holy Pope in Rome. The inscription reads,

23rd July 1949 Francis Rodriguez and Family Derby humbly beg the Apostolic Blessing and a Plenary Indulgence at the hour of death on condition that being truly sorry for their sins but unable to receive the last Sacraments they shall at least invoke with their lips and heart the Holy Name of Jesus.

It means that at the time of death, should any of our family not be in a position to be anointed, we would be blessed if we prayed in the name of Jesus. Dad cherished this award and it is one of the few items that remained among his possessions when he died in 2012. Perhaps it gave him a sense of fulfilment to know that his family would be taken care of in the spiritual world.

———

In contrast to the large, eye-catching Liveringa homestead high on a hill, Willumbah, 24 kilometres away, was the exact opposite. The stables and stockyards were built on flat ground while a few workers camped under the trees. Granny eventually moved there in August 1948 after Dad and Kim Rose built a house for them.

Willumbah outstation, Liveringa, 1950s. Source unknown

Her children stayed on with Aggie and Tom in Derby so the younger ones could go to school and the others remain in employment. They didn't see a lot of Granny after she moved to Willumbah, though Grampa visited them often enough on his trips to town. Aggie very likely felt a sense of duty to ensure that her siblings had a place to live. They respected her goodwill and helped with expenses and paid their rent. That she ran a tight ship was fine by them. Aggie always made sure her younger sisters had a chaperone when they went to dances, like the gentle but firm Bluegum Watson. She was cautious because there were a lot of soldiers around, leading Edna to reassure her older sister that they never got mixed up with them.

Jimmy and Leena attended the state school in Derby since there was no Catholic school. They had catechism lessons in the afternoons at the St John of God sisters' cottage, which had been their home since October 1945. The nuns had asked Bishop Raible for help to build a convent with the intention of combining it with a school. They reasoned that because a convent would be used for both purposes, the bishop should finance the building. He refused, probably because of financial constraints. He told them that while he could supply some building materials for a convent and they could use the church as their school, they should have the convent built at their own expense.

With no other option they took up the bishop's offer and opened their first classroom with twenty-one children in the nave of the church, separated from the altar with a curtain. Among the first students were my cousins Cyril and Pat Puertollano. There was no fanfare on opening day. Father Francis, the senior priest of the region, celebrated Benediction and then introduced the children to the principal, Sister Ignatius, who had been the head teacher at the Catholic school in Broome. With no resources the school nonetheless got underway and two weeks later essential teaching items began to arrive from Broome. It would be some time before the sisters found someone willing to build their convent.

Come holiday time the Fraser mob headed to Willumbah. The family loved being there. It was their place. With the camp mob, the children helped Grampa service windmills, saddle horses, chop wood and cook in camp ovens, and he showed them how to keep the meat fresh, by hanging waterbags on the inside of the meat house.

Grampa built the meat house at Willumbah using local timbers as the support beams and he stuffed spinifex between chicken mesh to form the walls. Spinifex had many uses. In its natural environment it prevented desert dunes from drifting, while Aboriginal people walled their shelters with it and they used its resin in spear making. Gudia, too, soon realised its potential. They used spinifex to bind mud walls of homesteads, as car tyre patches and to congeal temporary paths over creeks for their vehicles. Even sheep munched on its juicy flavours. A short distance away from the meat house were stables, stockyards and a work shed.

Leena, twenty years my Mum's junior, enjoyed unpacking the perishables that had arrived for Christmas from the monks at New Norcia – dried pears, apricots, peaches and wine wrapped in straw. The gifts affirmed Grampa's ongoing relationship with the Benedictines, while Dad also remained connected to the monks in more ways than one. He occasionally ordered a cache of wine from them.

Around this time, Frances decided to move on from her job at the Club Hotel to take up employment with Mr and Mrs Gillis

Coleman. Mrs Coleman had a kiosk and Frances really enjoyed the variety of work – making meat pies for picture nights, preparing iced lemon and raspberry squashes and baking bread. Gillis Coleman, in the days of no fridges, ran the powerhouse before it became a government concern. He made large ice blocks that people placed in iceboxes to keep their food cool. A forthright character, he rushed Frances to hospital the day she accidentally poured boiling water on herself. He was told to take her to the native hospital but he steadfastly refused and demanded the medical staff treat her immediately. Gillis Coleman saved Frances from severe burns and lifelong scarring. When the Colemans decided to move south, they asked her if she would like to go with them. She did, and in 1947 Frances moved to Perth.

The close-knit Frasers missed their sister and as soon as Edna had a chance, she followed. Her move to Perth as a mission-trained domestic was not unusual. The St John of God sisters found jobs for young mission-trained girls with gudia Catholic families in the city. Mrs O'Hara of Beaconsfield, the mother of seven boys whose husband was a horse trainer, had written to Father Francis in Broome looking for domestic help. Edna was offered the job and, with no hesitation, she accepted. Her Perth sojourn was a happy one in the O'Hara household, doing domestic chores. She boasted to me that she had even had her own room, that she sat at the same table and she wasn't treated any differently.

Gertie, too, took up a domestic's job in Perth. She was still a teenager when she went to live with Mrs and Dr Daley-Smith of Nedlands in the mid-1940s. They met her at the airport with two of their five daughters, Helia and Jocelyn. The Daley-Smith's daughters ranged in age from four months to thirteen years and Gertie, not much older than their eldest, looked after them. On arrival in Perth she was overwhelmed by the tall buildings, her head turning every which way at the sight of them. On Saturdays they all went to confession at a nearby church before heading to the beach for ice-creams, and at holiday times she went with the family to Esperance. Like Edna, Gertie enjoyed her Perth experience. She had two days off each week and on Thursdays she met with other mission girls in the city. Together they went shopping before hanging out at their common meeting place with a few young fullas in the Supreme Court Gardens. It is where Frances met Bill Ward.

Growing up in the county town of Katanning, 210 kilometres southeast of Perth, Bill's conservative family considered him to be the 'black sheep' of the family given his mates were mostly Noongars. A discerning young man, Bill Ward was only too aware of racist attitudes towards his mates in the town, and he became even more aware of racism after he met Frances. During WWII he was a home-guard patroller in the Perth suburb of Maylands before being sent to Noonkanbah, where he was in charge of artillery. When on R&R the army crew headed to Derby, staying in tents in Loch Street right near the Frasers' and Puertollanos' homes. Grampa took no chances, visiting the camp to warn the young men to stay away from his daughters.

Edna's Perth hiatus lasted just one year. Frances had given birth to Phillipa in June 1948 and she decided to travel to Derby to show her baby to the family, and Edna went with her. The trio disembarked at the Derby jetty from the SS *Koolinda* on 13 December 1948, the night that Aggie's youngest daughter,

Shirley, was born. After holidaying with the family, Frances returned to Perth with Phillipa and Edna stayed in Derby.

The Wards had three more children, Stanley, Anne and Charles. In 1955, around the time the youngest was born, Bill Ward became the curator of Queens Gardens in Perth and the family moved into the cottage on the site. They were well known to many Noongar people while countrimin from the Kimberley and other areas around the state were regular visitors to their home. Bill was an outspoken advocate and activist for the rights of Aboriginal people, and during the 1950s and '60s he would take his kids and Frances to the Esplanade on a Sunday, alongside the Derbal Yerrigan (Swan River), to take his turn on the soapbox at the Speakers Corner. The whole family participated in May Day marches. Bill had a strong social justice conscience and he was a member of the communist party. Their children, especially Phillipa, followed in his footsteps to be strong advocates for the rights of Aboriginal people in this state.

—

To my parents' delight, fifteen months after the birth of Pepita, a son came along on the 3rd of February 1951. They named him Francis James. In all likelihood, my brother's second name was after Mum's brother, Jimmy, and perhaps Nygumi. He became known as Franky.

While Mum's babies were born in a hospital, bush Aboriginal babies were not. They were delivered by Aboriginal midwives – in creek beds and under particular trees, as was Grampa and very likely Granny too. Patsy and Dickie Yambo's first son, Philip, was born in a dry creek bed near the shearers' quarters at Liveringa while their second child, Magdalene, arrived in the shearing shed at Myroodah when the family was there during Lore time. It was the wet season and they had walked to Myroodah carrying their food and swags. Patsy's remaining thirteen children were born in the Derby hospital after the family moved to town.

Perhaps motivated by the birth of a son, Dad became eager to have his own place and in 1951 he investigated buying a lease. He was keen to have a property beyond the Wunaamin Miliwundi (Leopold Ranges), some 200 kilometres northwest of Liveringa in Ngarinyin country. But when Kim Rose made him aware of a small KPC 54,000-acre lease called Backland Downs near Liveringa, he reconsidered and looked to the West Kimberley. The lease had previously been taken up by Campbell Dempster in 1937 and was returned to the Lands Department in 1943 because of a lack of any progress turning it into a pastoral property. It was pindan country, away from any river water source – hence its name – and in need of serious development. For my folks, Backland Downs was conveniently placed close to stable income opportunities, close to family at Willumbah and just 96 kilometres from Derby. On 24 January 1952 Dad signed a settlement with the KPC. Just seventy-three short years after Alexander Forrest reported good pasturelands in the region, my parents purchased their own lease for £27 6s rent per year. The KPC papers were officially signed by company directors John Forrest (the son of Alexander Forrest) and WEC McLarty. The deed was stamped with the common seal in the presence of the KPC board.

Filled with enthusiasm, Dad gathered together Grampa, Dicky and cousin Bewie to go with him and check out the lease. They made their way through the bush, over low shrub and spinifex from Willumbah to Backland Downs, where they found a bore and not much else. Dad renamed the lease Debesa, after the small feeding plots near his Galician home. After all, this 54,000-acre lease was small too, in comparison to most leases in the Kimberley. Debesa is where his sheep would feed and prosper. To Nigena people, this was Gnunda (tata lizard) country. The sandy pindan earth that is Debesa is besieged with the small lizards, along with other reptiles – barni, gerbada and snakes. Excited about having their own lease, Dad travelled regularly from Liveringa to Debesa. On a visit in January 1952 with Grampa and Jimmy Fraser, following decent rains, the countryside was looking great. It pleased them to find the swamp teeming with ducks and the sorghum that Dad had planted two weeks earlier sprouting. It would be several years before he and Mum would be in a position to relocate permanently to the property, though that didn't stop him from starting the homestead foundations.

Meanwhile, in the East Kimberley, on the back roads near Wyndham, agricultural scientist and visionary Kim Durack began eyeing the potential for crop growing on the upper Nigena lands of the Mardoowarra. He was a grandson of the pioneering pastoralist Patsy Durack of Argyle Station. In the previous decade, after the Durack family's many years of unprofitable cattle exploits in the East Kimberley, Durack had investigated new ideas for their properties. He had already realised the potential for irrigation pastures in the Ord River valley during the mid-1940s along with his brother William. The two had successfully grown sorghum and millet. When their father, Michael Durack, sold their East Kimberley properties, he felt let down but not defeated. With the same vision Kim Durack looked to the West Kimberley, to the Mardoowarra floodplains, to continue his research.

In 1951 he began negotiations with the KPC in Perth. He wanted to experiment growing rice alongside Uralla Creek a few kilometres from the Liveringa homestead and close to Willumbah. He was a friend of Kim Rose, which is probably why he was able to get support from the company as he went about securing backing from government and private interests for his project. The result was that 10,000 acres were excised from the Liveringa lease, despite it being the best lambing area on the station. The research farm was named Camballin.

In Perth, Durack organised the necessary equipment and supplies to be sent up to Camballin and, with his sister Elizabeth, he set off on the 7th of November 1952 for his new venture. Towing a purpose-built caravan that he named Miss Kimberley, the pair travelled in a Ford truck. His plan was to sow fields of rice on the floodplains between the high ground and Uralla Creek. Durack strategically positioned Miss Kimberley overlooking the Mardoowarra floodplains, not far from where Grampa was born.

The area was potentially ideal to grow rice. Almost free of trees and shrubs were fields of natural grasses, which I imagine would once have been harvested and placed in 'stooks' as a food resource by Nigena people. Now Durack claimed that the clay was well suited to growing rice because it could hold water during the wet season. But the shortcomings lay in the floodplains not being able to hold water during the dry. Despite adequate rainfall in the upper catchment of the river, by midyear it had stopped flowing. For the rice-growing scheme to be successful, Kim Durack realised that irrigation was necessary. He encountered many problems that affected the crop yield, including the unpredictability of floods. Some years the waters rose high, even flooding the area where he camped, while other years he waited and waited for floods that never came, as in the 1951–52 season, which was recorded as being the driest in fifty years.

Durack studied the water levels, experimented with varieties of rice and grasses and, with a shotgun in hand, fought off the bird life that took a liking to the new pastures. The magnificent northern Australian water cranes, the 'native companion', better known as the brolga, that had danced and fed on the river's floodplains for millennia proved to be the most destructive perennial pest of all. Durack did eventually succeed in convincing the Western Australian government to direct the Public Works Department to implement a suitable irrigation system.

———

In April the following year on a visit to the paddy fields, Kim Durack asked Dad if he was interested in working at Camballin. He was only too aware of Dad's reputation and Mum's cooking capabilities. He then wrote to the Secretary of Northern Developments, his employer in Sydney, advising the company that he intended to employ a married couple on a permanent basis. He went on to say that the man he had in mind was held in high esteem throughout the country for his abilities.

Within a few weeks Dad was working at Camballin – closer to Willumbah and closer to Debesa. With his offsider, Chook Fowler, he built whatever Durack wanted. Sheds, cottages, outbuildings and a poultry yard. He also worked in the rice field and laid the foundations for a shed that would become his family's temporary home, later to be replaced by a cottage he built as our permanent home. Attached to the cottage was a flywire-enclosed mess and kitchen that Mum worked from.

The Mardoowarra landscape, of grassed floodplains set between distant hills and the river, was changing. Irrigation channels, 8 feet wide, were dug into the rich soil from which fields of green rice stalks waved in the breeze at their European farmers. Gone were the natural grasses that had been nurtured and developed over a very long time by Nigena people. Now zenith rice, the variety of rice considered suitable for northern conditions, was flourishing across the floodplains. Dad took a keen interest in Durack's research. As the rice crops sprouted, he was reminded of the fields of produce at Freixo. The plants turned yellow and the parched soil turned to chunks of crusty grey mud. Dad relished the opportunity to nurture them when his boss was away on business trips in Perth and Sydney.

Mum, heavily pregnant, relocated to Derby while Granny and Grampa together with Dottie and her baby daughter Kerry, just six weeks older than me, helped Dad look after Pepita, four and a half years old, and Franky, three. Kerry was raised by our grandparents after her mum went to Darwin in search of work and stayed. Growing up on Willumbah, she had always heard that Grampa had Walmajarri heritage as well as Nigena, which has left us wondering if our great-grandmother Brumby may have come to live with Nigena people when her country was taken over by pastoralists for their stock. With no paper trail for many 'full-descent' people, we will never know for sure.

The women at Willumbah helped Granny look after Kerry, carting her around in a coolamon (wooden carrying vessel). On a visit home to Derby in the late 1970s, she was gifted that very coolamon by an extended Nigena family who had kept it safe for her all those years. Now it takes pride of place in Kerry's Darwin home.

Kerry's coolamon, rested on wild passionfruit vines, Darwin, 2019
© *Kevin McCarthy, photographer*

I arrived on Saturday, the 27th of June 1953, in the Derby hospital. It would be years later, when I ordered a birth certificate, that I discovered my official name was Mary Therese Jacintha [sic] and not Jacinta Therese, the name I had always known. I am chuffed, nonetheless, that Dad mentioned my birth in his diary:

> *This morning Katie gave birth to the fourth child, and both well*
> *Thank God. I left here today after dinner with the two little ones*

*Pepita and Franky. Also the old man Fraser. We arrived in the
evening in Derby, and today went and see Katie in the hospital.*

As the year drew to a close, Mum and Dad settled into life at
Camballin. She as the cook while looking after us kids and Dad
sometimes worked at Liveringa. At every possible moment
he travelled to Debesa to progress the lease. From November
that year Kimberley people watched with anticipation as the
build-up to the wet produced patchy storm clouds that rolled in
from the east, with little or no rain. On their seventh wedding
anniversary, Dad took all of us to Derby and to holy mass. He
purchased a windmill and we returned to Camballin via Debesa.
This way of life became routine.

Dad was pleased that the station now had two windmills
pumping fresh, sweet water into the tanks. It was particu-
larly pleasing because in 1953 there was little rain in the
West Kimberley, though decent falls further east filled the
Mardoowarra tributaries that flowed downstream to Camballin.
The flood ran a bank at the Uralla Bridge that year, flooding the
fields to the delight of the rice-growing research team.

The year wound up with a Christmas party at Camballin
with managers, employees and their families from Liveringa and
Willumbah. Kim Durack and the Rose family then left for their
holidays down south, countrimin headed to ceremonial sites
on nearby stations, Granny and Grampa waited at Willumbah
for the family to arrive from Derby, and Mum and Dad busied
themselves between Camballin and Debesa.

CHAPTER 5

A sense of place

*The Johnston crocs seemed unperturbed by the
swimming and splashing in the creeks*

At the end of a one-mile track off the main road between
Derby and Fitzroy Crossing, the Debesa homestead was
emerging. A two-wheel track weaved its way through spinifex,
wattle and kungerberry (sweet berry) bushes over gnunuda
terrain. In 1953 a makeshift homestead set in soft pindan among
scrub was nothing more than a tent and a bough shed nuzzled
next to a windmill. Despite being a long way from any river
watercourses, by the end of the year Dad was pleased with the
two windmills that pumped good-quality water into the tanks.
As the station progressed over the years, each windmill was
named after one of his family or someone who had a connection
with Debesa. The first was called Pepitas. This was our place.

In the early 1950s a gravel main road between Derby and
Fitzroy Crossing opened, replacing the track that ran close to the
river and through the Liveringa homestead where Dad observed
the comings and goings of travellers and visitors. Now the new

road improved access between the two towns, though it was still vulnerable to flooding and closure during the wet. Travellers could be stranded for up to three weeks on either side of a flooded crossing, like at Hardman Creek west of Fitzroy Crossing.

Mum and Dad were conveniently placed at Camballin and remained there for the time being, while Kim Durack set out to have a mansion built on the edge of the floodplains. He contracted two Italian builders to build a Greek-style home that he called the 'Parthenon'. But the Italians' contract was short-lived as life in remote Australia took its toll. They suffered culture shock, experienced language difficulties and found the heat unbearable. Both soon became fatigued and sick, and by early 1954 they had returned to Perth. Work on the Parthenon had hardly begun and now any plans lay in abeyance. An arch that was intended to adorn the end of the roof lay alongside building materials and a pile of river stones gathering dust as Durack contemplated what to do next. Dad reckoned part of the problem was because Durack was short of finance.

———

Like the principal homestead at Liveringa in the previous decade, Willumbah was often abuzz with activity. It was home to several people, including the mob in the camp, while the close-knit Fraser siblings came from Derby whenever they could.

Willumbah is a special place for all of us, embedded deep in our psyche. Willumbah is where Granny and Grampa had made their home on country – Nigena country. Located near the present-day Inkarta feedlots, its far-reaching floodplains that stretch across the landscape remain firmly embedded in our oral histories. Of greyish-brown soil and carpeted with fields of ribbon-like grasses, the plains soak up the rains during the wet. As the season came to an end, the soil turned to pasty clay potholes under the weight of sheep, goats and horses' hooves. By the time the dry season arrived, deep cracks had formed and the soil crumbled like powder in your hand.

The Willumbah homestead was made of standard corrugated-iron walls and cement floors with asbestos panels separating the kitchen from a huge room where most everyone slept. The grandkids loved that room. It had plenty of space for camp beds and swags scattered around that spilled out onto the verandahs. In the yard, oleander and hibiscus plants struggled to survive despite plenty of watering and sheep's manure spread around the roots.

During the day, people in the camp mingled under a couple of bough sheds, but by nightfall they had lugged their swags closer to the house. Most evenings Granny and Grampa said the rosary and invited them – but there was never any pressure. Grampa never tried to force his Western religion on anyone. He had a good understanding of his countrimin's beliefs, customs and ceremonial commitments on country. My oldest cousin, Cyril Puert, as we called him, learned from Grampa that when it was ceremony time, it was proper to ensure bush people had extra rations.

At the same time, my grandparents had great faith in the healing abilities of the learned medicine men in the camp, like old Jerry, who lived there with his wife Amy and daughter Aggie. Granny was beside herself with worry one evening when Grampa became awfully sick with stomach aches, and she went with him to see Jerry. He had Grampa lie on a swag and, as he worked over his stomach, pulling hair from his navel, the old man sang to Grampa. The pains subsided and he was able to go home and rest.

The Fraser siblings got along well, as did their children. Our solidarities could only have pleased Granny and Grampa. Our loyalty to each other had grown from their experiences of being snatched from their immediate families. Confused as young children, they themselves kept their own children close for fear of losing them in the same way. The removal and disruption of our people by governments and missionaries was the catalyst that kept families together after they left the missions, as they adjusted to living in non-Aboriginal societies they had had little experience with.

Most every holiday time Aggie with her children headed to Willumbah. If Tom couldn't take them, they hitched a ride with locals, usually family or friends like Jim Ishiguchi on his loading truck, or with Dave Bickley in his taxi. Dave, who at one time was a head drover with his own plant and team mustering cattle south along the Canning Stock Route, did a lot of that, driving people to stations and even to Broome.

Sometimes it seemed that everyone was at Willumbah. Mum, Aggie, Gertie, Edna, Dottie, Jimmy, Leena, their spouses and an increasing bevy of grandchildren. There was plenty to keep everyone busy and interested. Together with the camp kids, the older grandchildren headed to the stockyards to help round up the sheep, clean troughs and milk the goats. They loved the stables and stockyards. Hanging over the rails they were capti-vated by the stockmen who fed, groomed and saddled up horses.

Cheering as Grampa shot a killer (sheep), they watched as he hung and butchered it in the meat house, making sure there was enough for everyone at Willumbah.

Holiday time was free range for the kids. Every day they disappeared into the bush to collect magabalas, kungerberries and ngili-ngilis and to climb boab trees looking for rainwater trapped in the cavities. They cracked open boab nuts to eat the dry pulp, then during the wet when the water lilies bloomed in the swamps, they swam down to pick the root bulbs off the white flowers, leaving the smaller purple and yellow ones to mature. Cooked on the coals or boiled in a billy, the bulbs peeled easily like a yam, and seasoned with salt and pepper they even tasted like sweet potato. On the down side, swimming in man-made dams had its shortcomings – leeches clung to juicy little legs and arms to suck blood from their victims.

Cyril Puert loved the bush and everything it offered a young man. He was close in age to his uncle Jimmy Fraser and the two got along well. They helped with burn-offs before the wet set in, 'all the way to Erskine Ranges from Willumbah,' Cyril grinned. Proper young firebugs, those two. They jumped on and off the cart, setting fire to the spinifex while yelling to Grampa to get the old horse Biddy to pull the cart faster. It was an irony really. Here they were, practising the long-standing Aboriginal custom of fire-stick farming that encouraged sustenance regrowth for human consumption. Now the regrowth was the fresh fodder for introduced animals that had taken over our ancestors' lands. The boys loved nothing more than running through the scrub and over mudflats to kill birds with their shanghais and with Grampa's pea rifle.

Sustenance-packed floodplains and creeks were Willumbah's bush pantries. Men hunted bush turkey and barni (goanna) and everyone went fishing. The river and creeks were abundant with barramundi, catfish, jarrambas, shark, stingray and swordfish. When heading to the creek, some hitched a ride on the cart rather than walk over the potholes. It was worth the long trek to Uralla Creek where the Johnston crocs seemed unperturbed by the swimming and splashing in the creeks. As little kids we learned to catch jarramba by tying a baited thread to the end of a long stick and dangling it in the creek until we felt a nibble – then quickly flicking our catch onto the bank. The older girls sat in the shallows of the river under shady trees holding their skirts out under the water. When jarrambas swam over their skirts, they folded in their catch. Cooked in a billy of salted boiling water, jarrambas were peeled and seasoned with salt and vinegar – every last morsel savoured.

Horse riding didn't appeal much to the town kids. Cyril didn't like riding, unlike Jimmy and Leena, who eased into stock life. Leena even aspired to being a jillaroo. But if Aggie's youngest daughter, Shirley, ever had any desire to become a stockwoman, it ended right there at Willumbah the day she hopped on a horse: 'I nearly died of fright. That was out at Nemile where Grampa was bringing in the sheep ... it kept on going towards a branch and I nearly got my bloody neck cut off.'

Grampa trained young gudia jackaroos in stock work on Liveringa. They came from Broome and from Perth and they called him, simply, Fraser. Unlike Jimmy, who was schooled in Derby, these young men went to prestigious Perth colleges, yet it was Jimmy who was the capable teenage stockman. During flood times when the rains topped up the tributaries that connected to the Mardoowarra, he was busy preventing sheep from drowning in the floods. Grampa prepared crude rafts for them by pushing logs together and tying them with thin, twine-like bark from bush fig trees. Together with eight or so camp lads Jimmy forced sheep up into the sand hills to safety. They stayed with the sheep for a couple of weeks, until the waters subsided. Massive volumes of water twisted and gushed from the northern reaches of the river system and raced past Liveringa to Yeeda before emptying into the sea, while floodplains along the way guzzled generous amounts of water.

In 1954 Dad began stocking Debesa with sheep. His application for a dedicated earmark was approved and he received a Certificate of Registration of Stock Brands. He bought a flock of twenty sheep for £1 each from Jeff Rose, Kim's relative, at Quanbun Downs Station. The Kimberley had had a late wet that year and it took him five days to cart the sheep the 70 kilometres over sloppy dirt roads from Quanbun to Debesa. Torrential downpours scoured the roads, forming potholes that filled with mud and dried into soft, fine bull dust. Driving over a pothole filled with bull dust had the potential to damage tyres and wheel rims. When Dad's truck got bogged he corralled the sheep and it took a day for the road to dry out enough for him to work his truck out of the bog.

West Kimberley people were used to travelling over dirt roads. In the days when the main track ran alongside the river connecting the stations, it could only be used in the dry season.

From when the Kimberley first opened up for pastoralism, the means of getting cattle to port varied over time. First, there were drovers who mustered stock to Derby and Broome along routes that followed the river. They rested and watered their stock where the droving passage caressed windmills and waterholes, courtesy or not, of sheep stations. But the long haul took its toll. While the livestock may have left in good condition, by the time they reached the Derby port, often several months later, their condition had deteriorated. The animals had lost weight, were weary and some died, all of which resulted in poor sales.

The problem was solved momentarily in the 1950s, at least for some in the northern Kimberley, when an innovative scheme to 'air' beef commenced at Glenroy Station. An abattoir was built and Dad was contracted to undertake formwork during the construction phase. The beef was packed on site and then freighted in aircraft fitted with refrigeration to Wyndham for export. The scheme was not cost-effective, however. While it relied heavily on government funding, only stations in the immediate area benefited from it. Consequently, the Western Australian government turned to the Commonwealth to help grow the beef industry and they obliged by improving the roads.

The improved roads coincided with the advent of high-powered road trains. Travelling over dirt roads with tight bends, the cattle were delivered battered and bruised and still at a loss of income for the pastoralists. But the upside to improved roads was that they enhanced the mobility of station people in general and it benefited sheep stations in getting wool to port.

—

By November 1954 Dad had laid the foundations for a home-stead at Debesa. There was no urgency because he couldn't see the family moving there in the foreseeable future. He inlaid the cement floors with river stones from Camballin that Grampa and his young helpers, Jimmy and Leena, had selected. As Debesa slowly progressed Dad continued to source an income on nearby stations and in Derby. At times he took the whole family with him on jobs. It wasn't unusual to find Mum and us kids camped near a mill while he had gone into Derby to collect parts and stores. We did a lot of travelling around the area. Always on the move, back and forth between Myroodah and Noonkanbah and Lulugui and Liveringa.

Meantime, the St John of God sisters found themselves in a position to have their convent built in Derby and they approached Dad. He agreed but couldn't settle on a start date immediately. They would have to wait for an opportune time as he continued to fulfil commitments on his various jobs, including his own priorities at Debesa.

Jimmy had already turned fifteen by January 1955 when he started working with Dad. As the two were preparing a small paddock at Debesa to plant kapok, Kim Durack turned up. He came to ask Dad whether he would build his mansion. It had been two years since the Italian builders reneged on their contract and Dad knew that there was no other stonemason in the region. He agreed.

On 27th of February he and Jimmy started on the walls of Durack's Parthenon. Dad called it the 'stone house'. With limited money on the part of the Northern Land Development, it would be a smaller version of what Durack had envisaged.

He paid Dad £100 a month, or whenever he had money, from which Dad paid Jimmy his wages. 'There was no big money from Durack for that building,' Dad bemoaned as I sat and interviewed him and Jimmy on the back verandah of Gertie's Darwin home in August 2003.

The Camballin construction site, 1955 © Frank Rodriguez, photographer

While some materials were supplied, most of the building was made from river sand and stones. Dad carted it all with his truck to the site. A hard worker, he laboured tirelessly on that house. He worked long hours, often in stifling heat, and young Jimmy was expected to do the same.

For almost three years they worked together at Debesa and at Camballin. Dad taught Jimmy to make bricks with a small hand-mixer. 'Those corner bricks. Yeah, I must have made hundreds,' Jimmy chimed in as he looked to the sky thoughtfully. They moulded large colonnades and poured cement into the pillar frames as the stone house began to take shape. Two more builders came on site to help: Pat Begley, a young chap who had just completed a carpenter's apprenticeship in Perth and had headed north to earn some money and gain experience; and an Englishman, John Hall. Both men kept in touch with Dad over the years.

A steady stream of Durack's family and friends visited the site, taking photographs and being generally interested in the progress. Among the visitors was Horrie Miller, a Western Australian aviator and co-founder of MacRobertson Miller Airlines (MMA) who was married to the writer Mary Durack, Kim's sister. A member of the Rose inner circle, Miller was impressed with Dad's work ethic and his workmanship and was aware that the Spaniard had bought the small lease once attached to Liveringa.

Durack's emerging 'Parthenon', Camballin, 1957. Frank is on the far right. Source unknown

In March Dad bought another seventy sheep, this time from Noonkanbah, increasing his flock to ninety just before shearing time. For his first ever muster Dad borrowed horses from Grampa at Willumbah. Mustering presented him with an unexpected challenge because the backcountry was virtually impassable. With the wet over, it meant that the fast-growing feathertop threeawn grass, with seeds that resembled spearheads, was 6 feet high and making it difficult to find the sheep. He found only seven. Alarmed, his mind travelled back to his childhood, falling asleep in the warm, grassy fields near Norcedas and waking to find the cows gone. He remembered being punished with no tea until they were found. Now at Debesa the adult shepherd had lost his own sheep. To his relief they emerged in small clusters from the scrub in the ensuing days.

For the first shearing time at Debesa, Dad borrowed a plant and a shearer for a day from Liveringa. Seventy-four sheep were shorn then and in the following days he completed the job by shearing the stragglers himself. He had to be an all-rounder – shearer, roustabout and wool classer. Throwing the fleece onto a makeshift sorting table, he tore off the dangling, matted locks of wool, rolled the fleece into a tight bundle and jammed it into a large wool bale. Once tightly secured with metal clamps he proudly stamped the very first consignment of four bales with the Debesa brand. Loaded and secured onto his truck, he headed to the Derby wharf. Sheep numbers increased over time and mustering became more manageable as the sheep munched their way through the dense scrub, stunting the growth of the backcountry for the lifespan of the sheep station.

—

Mum was pregnant again when she moved to Derby from Camballin with us kids in 1955. This time her pregnancy was not going smoothly so Dad put building operations at Camballin on hold to be with her. She was admitted to hospital on a couple of occasions before my brother Phillip John arrived on the 26th of May. Coincidently, it was the feast day of St Philip Neri, the patron saint of Rome, of the US Special Forces, of humour and of joy. Moreover, St Philip's father's name just happened to be Francesco. Was my brother named after this saint? I don't know. What I do know is that baby Phillip was rushed by RFDS to Perth with 'blue baby syndrome' or anoxemia – a condition caused by a defect that prevents the heart from receiving enough oxygen. The baby was successfully treated and he returned home one week later.

As I read through my father's diaries, I often wondered how he ever managed to fit everything in. He found work about town doing construction jobs and on the wharf, yet he made time to progress Debesa. Most weekends he returned to Camballin to work on the stone house. Despite Dad's necessary interruptions, Kim Durack was delighted with the progress on the stone house. He wrote to the Northern Land Development, saying that Frank Rodriguez was doing a magnificent job and, in his opinion, he was the only person in the country who could do it.

Living in Derby through this period proved to be an opportune time to build the convent, and Dad spent long hours on the building. It took him just three months. For church-related work Dad only ever charged a nominal fee yet he still contributed a percentage of his weekly earnings towards the upkeep of the church in the two collections at Sunday masses, as required under canon law.

My mother turned thirty-five on the 24th of November 1955, the day we returned to Camballin. With the baby in a cot beside her, Mum returned to work in the kitchen while my older siblings helped to look after me. They often played by the creek collecting small crabs that they gleefully let loose on the cottage floor. Andy Miller, Horrie's son and Durack's nephew, sometimes spent the school holidays at Camballin where, among other things, he taught my siblings to trap birds and steal eggs from their nests. There was never a dull moment when Andy Miller was around. One time, as they all walked towards the rice paddies with me in the pram, he yelled, 'Elephant!' and pointed to a dead, fly-blown donkey lying in the floodplains across the small timber bridge. Terrified, the three abandoned the pram and ran back to Mum in the kitchen.

'Where's Jacinta?' They couldn't tell her. Mum ran to the bridge where the pram's wheel had become jammed in the timber crossing with me still inside. And here I am today, alive and well to tell my families' stories.

Christmas wasn't far off and Mum was happy to be home with the family. It rained that year, turning the road into a quagmire, and the only sure way to get to Camballin for the party from Willumbah was by horse and cart. Grampa loaded everyone onto the cart and off they went, Tom and Aggie and my cousins. Shirley came without a party dress so Mum pulled out her treadly and whipped up two matching dresses, one for Shirley and one for Pepita. The festivities were held under the boab tree next to Kim Durack's caravan, adorned with lights, in the front yard of the stone house. The next day us Fraser mob headed to Willumbah to continue the celebrations. Grampa dressed up as Father Christmas but his idea of what Santa looked like was different to anyone else's and he frightened the children so much we screamed, running away from him. Creeping through the few trees on the edge of the floodplain dressed in a gown with a dark hood and carrying a straw broom, he looked more like a sorceress.

I was just three years old in March 1956 when Mum suffered a partial stroke and was rushed to the Derby hospital. It's my earliest clear memory. I can still see her face – distorted and sad. She was not well. 'What's wrong with Mummy?' I asked, bewildered. But no-one seemed to notice me. It's probably why I tried to get a better view of what was going on and toppled headfirst into a sawn-off 44-gallon drum of dry cement. I distinctly remember her sitting up in the passenger seat of a truck and Dad handing ten-month-old Phillip to Kim Durack in the driver's seat. She spent the next two months in town, in and out of hospital until the doctors were satisfied that she could go home.

As mustering time approached, Dad put the stone house on hold and headed to Debesa to undertake his small but significant shearing program. Every year Mum's extended family were there to help and each year the tally of bales increased. One hundred and six sheep were shorn, and sixteen lambs tailed and earmarked in 1956. Dad then bought one hundred ewes from Ellendale Station.

It was June when Dad and Jimmy returned to work on the stone house, though not before helping Durack sow the rice crop. With an intermittent work schedule, it took them two years to complete. With Dad's absences from Debesa the station was left exposed, which caused him anguish. Dingoes killed lambs, while exploration companies bulldozed seismic tracks through the property, downing fences without resetting them. On one occasion thieves stole shearing bits, tools and a petrol pump. Dad had his suspicions as he took matters into his own hands after reporting the theft to the police. He confronted the Bell Brothers' workers, who were contracted to WAPET to grade the seismic tracks – they returned a petrol pump, but no tools. As for the dingoes, he dealt with them with poisoned bait like he had at Liveringa, but now he also set deadly jaw traps, buried in the loose earth with a clump of meat nestled on top. The habitually crafty dingoes were vulnerable around readily available meat.

Dominic and Katie Rodriguez, Debesa, 1960s © Frank Rodriguez, photographer

To continue stocking his lease with no stable cash flow, Dad partook in a form of goods exchange that can be best described as 'personal goods barter'. Large sheep stations surrounded his small lease, therefore bargaining in this way suited him. He could make a profit from the wool off the sheep that he had swapped for his building expertise. It seems to have been a reasonable arrangement for him, but it wasn't necessarily fair. By bartering, Dad avoided the cost of buying sheep while bigger station managers were underhanded. In April 1957 he entered into an arrangement with Jeff Rose at Quanbun. Dad built and cemented a tank in exchange for one thousand wethers, but Jimmy Fraser was unimpressed with some managers' tactics: 'They'd give him sheep with cancer ears. He'd have to cut all the ears off. But he took them, and we ended up getting some good wool out of them.'

Bartering was never entered into between my parents' family and friends. Helping each other was unconditional. Mutual arrangements were par for the course in our sphere. My parents visited Grampa, even when he was out in the lamb-tailing camp, and Grampa helped out at Debesa. My grandparents' goodwill and support is how Dad initially managed the lease. He worked on Grampa's vehicle or took Granny and Grampa and the kids wherever they needed to go. They helped him with the children when Mum wasn't there. During mustering time Grampa was at Debesa to help out, and he put in miles of fencing with Dad and helped carry out maintenance on the windmills. Sometimes Tony and Ellen Ozies checked in on Debesa when no-one was there. Dad was grateful and pleased they gathered tasty watermelons that had sprung from seeds he had tossed around the windmills.

My Dad's strong work ethic never faltered. He was constantly on the go. Sometimes too busy to make entries in his diary, he would catch up at the end of the month. Ten years after he built the Holy Rosary Church, he mentions building a stone wall in the front of the church. That wall remains today as part of the front yard of the Catholic presbytery. Well into the 1950s Derby's Catholic parish continued to expand. One hundred and eighty parishioners lived in Derby alone, with another one hundred at Bungarun, while twenty-seven pupils attended the Catholic school run by the St John of God sisters. A new outdoor classroom with wooden benches wedged into the earthen floor and topped with a spinifex roof created more space outside of the improvised church classroom. Mum and Dad were eager that us kids received a Catholic education beyond what they themselves had and it is the reason they moved into their Stanley Street state house in 1957. Pepita began her schooling in the outdoor classroom that year. Our families lived near each other, with Aggie and Tom in Loch Street that ran at an angle to Stanley Street, and Leena, now with two toddlers and married to Alfie Buckle, lived in Delawarr Street directly behind our place.

Prospects for missionaries received a boost in 1957 when the state government allocated land in Derby for two 'native' hostels. Both the United Aborigines Mission and the Pious Society of Missions Incorporated (the Catholic Church) had been selected for 'native purposes'. The missionaries were to provide suitable accommodation for students to attend primary, secondary and technical schools in the town. The hostels were to be built opposite each other, on the corners of Alphonsas and Ashley streets, and Wodehouse and Ashley streets.

Father Joe Kearney, Derby's parish priest, contracted Dad to build the Catholic hostel. His brief was to have it completed in time for the start of the 1959 school year and construction began on 14 May 1958. Carpenters Pat Begley, Brian Flynn and later Bob Jodrell joined Dad in reaching that target. The trio of offsiders camped at the construction site and had their meals at our home, always complimenting Mum's cooking.

Constructing the hostel came with challenges. Not only did the builders find it difficult to dig into the hard, red earth, the hostel was being built on a slope that posed alignment problems. Furthermore, the Boucher-designed frame that had been built to specifications in Perth arrived with the ceiling joists 4 inches off centre. Notwithstanding these setbacks and given the era and distance from Perth, the hostel was on track to be completed on time.

St Joseph's Hostel, Derby, 1959 © Frank Rodriguez, photographer

Debesa was never off Dad's mind. He found time to barter and on weekends he headed out to the station, sometimes with the carpenters who helped him progress the homestead. Dad's enthusiasm to develop his property never waned. He was in his element as he worked the small lease. Mum always supported him as he grew the station, while she cared for all of us despite her own health slowly deteriorating.

———

Horrie Miller had begun to show an interest in Debesa in 1957. Realising the inevitability of bigger airline companies taking over smaller companies like his, Miller had moved to the Kimberley in the mid-1940s with the idea of finding a replacement business. As the self-imposed regional manager for MMA, he managed the northern ports and lived mostly in Broome. A tall man with a stooped stature, a rather large pointed nose, protruding chin and thin receding grey hair, he always seemed to wear a slight grin. The Broome townspeople liked Horrie Miller, a generous man who didn't mind supporting local community groups. He had six children, some of whom spent holidays with him. Mary Durack, too, sometimes lived in Broome. But given her profession as a historian and writer, she generally stayed in Perth with her children – closer to libraries, relevant resources and suitable schools.

In the early 1950s Mr Miller, as we called him, had already investigated the possibility of leasing Dampier Downs, a dilapidated sheep station north of Broome. The lease had no stock but there were plenty of wild donkeys and dingoes. It had been on the market since the Depression years. He and Mary tried living there for a while but, with no farming background, it was a hopeless situation for them both. After six months he abandoned the lease but not, it seems, the idea of having a well-managed small property in the Kimberley.

Twenty years Dad's senior, Miller approached my father in Derby about going into business together. Miller was well aware that the hard-working Spaniard with an Aboriginal wife and four young children was developing his small lease with no financial backing. Dad was cautious, as he suspected there was another reason Miller was keen to negotiate with him. It seems that because Miller knew his brother-in-law Kim Durack had struggled to pay Dad properly for the stone house, his offer might have had something to do in the way of compensating Dad. Nonetheless, Miller's proposition appealed to the ambitious thirty-seven year old eager to establish his pastoral property. Surely, having an apparent successful businessman in the mix could be beneficial. The proposition had potential.

Mr Miller visited Dad often throughout 1958, arriving unexpectedly at Debesa and on building sites in Derby. With him on some occasions was Cyril Gare, MMA's secretary and Miller's friend and confidante. Gare was also the accountant for Miller's private company, Miller Investments. Cyril Gare provides an interesting adjunct to this story, given his close involvement with Aboriginal peoples in the southwest. Given that my Dad was never comfortable with the accountant, I did some research into the man.

In 1952 the Native Welfare Council was formed to help assimilate Noongars down south. One of its members was none other than Cyril Gare, who became its president in 1957.

During the 1960s the organisation became the Aboriginal Advancement Council and its focus was on supporting south-west Aboriginal people to adjust to white society. The Council remained closely aligned with the Department of Native Welfare and wudjella (non-Aboriginal) humanitarians were intent on teaching Noongars to live like them. It was post-war Western Australia and Aboriginals' perceived plight was receiving a lot of attention.

Volunteers offered advice on housekeeping, budgeting, parenting and encouraging kids to go to school. By the mid-1960s there were twenty-five organisations that came under the umbrella of the Advancement Council with Gare at its helm. It was around this time that Horrie Miller and Cyril Gare approached Dad about going into partnership. Interestingly, then, for the duration of the Miller/Rodriguez partnership, Gare was not only Miller Investments' accountant, but he also headed up a significant Aboriginal affairs organisation in Perth.

Cyril Gare was a domineering official and the all-white council was not without its infighting. They jostled for control and power while advocating for the rights of Aboriginals. Few Noongars made any attempt to gain positions within those organisations because they didn't regard themselves as being like white, middle-class Australians. They generally refused to bow to white supremacy. Neither did they accept being pushed towards white goals and they avoided becoming members of organisations formed in, supposedly, their best interests.

In the late 1960s southwest Aboriginals were being encouraged to fill positions on the council and Gare found himself a suitable contender in Jack Davis. Originally from the north of the state but reared in the south, Davis had established himself as a poet and he possessed a flair for mixing with white people. Gare became Davis's main supporter and endorsed him as president of the Aboriginal Advancement Council.

When Gare stepped down in 1970 it is unlikely that either of my parents had any idea of his role outside of being Horrie Miller's bookkeeper. I am left to speculate as to whether his style and attitude influenced the way he managed Debesa's books. Did Gare harbour a similar perception about an interracial, marginalised family in the West Kimberley? My father never warmed to him.

Despite not having any grounding in stock work, Miller was well connected. My father, on the other hand, lacked any business identity, yet he was a capable station manager. Pat Begley, meanwhile, who by this time had gone into partnership with Dad, was keen to let go of his share. Begley's interests were in the south and Miller could take over his one-third share. In early 1958 Dad and Miller agreed to go into business together and Miller Investments worked on the finer details. Miller wrote to Cyril Gare on 10 February that year,

> *I have just read through the agreement. The part about Clause II will have to be altered, as it may not be possible for F. Rodriguez to devote his whole time to the working of the property, and it might even be a disadvantage, as he can do certain work which is in demand by other neighbouring stations, from time to time and get paid with sheep. Also his family have to be provided for and if there is not sufficient return from the station, he will have to seek some means to keep them. The clause which would give H. Miller*

> *control and management of the policy of the partnership could also*
> *be altered, as Rodriguez is the senior partner and has the better*
> *knowledge of how to work the property. This could come under*
> *ordinary agreement between the partners on the best ways and*
> *means.*

Miller held an optimistic view that small landowners could be successful, as no doubt did Dad. They agreed for Dad to have a two-thirds share in the partnership and Miller one-third, taking over Begley's stake. Towards the end of 1958 the pair signed the Debesa lease. Begley was paid £750 cash on 31 October and Dad and Miller commenced their partnership on 1 November. My parents could now move to Debesa sooner rather than later.

———

In late 1958 relatives from Spain started to arrive in Australia. Dad's nephew and our first cousin, Jose Vazquez, was the first of several. We called him Joe. He had arrived in Australia with his younger brother Julio the previous year to work in the cane fields in Queensland. Both were eager to meet their tio (uncle) so Dad had little trouble enticing them to come and work in the rice fields at Camballin. It was New Year's Eve when Dad loaded us kids onto the back of his Chev truck and headed to the Derby airport. Joe's arrival was the perfect Christmas present. Dad had not seen any of his family for over two decades. In English and Spanish, muddled blissful words spilled into his diary, 'Mi sobrini (my nephew) arrived here from Queensland. This is the first time I have met any of my family after 21 years of haven't seen any of them from anywhere. Grande Navedad

(Wonderful Christmas).' He then drove Joe around Derby showing off his small town before taking him to see Debesa. Julio would follow in February.

November to December of 1958 was an especially busy time. On the 19th of November, as Dad travelled along the main road towards Debesa, he was pulled over – as station people were in the days before telephones – by the manager of Noonkanbah Station, Duncan Beaton. He asked Dad if he would build a cottage in Derby for the Country Women's Association. They would pay him £999. Dad agreed. Not only was he fast-tracking his home-stead, he was on target to complete St Joseph's Hostel in time for the new school year, and now he would build the CWA cottage.

Dad discussed design options with Mrs Henwood of Calwynyardah who, when satisfied, gave the go-ahead for the project. Keen to have a staging house in town, gudia station people constantly came on site to check on the progress, while Mrs Beaton – Duncan Beaton's wife – strutted around with her three daughters in tow, giving Dad instructions about the design. Brian Flynn came over from the hostel to work on the cottage. Then, with Joe helping, Dad completed cementing the hostel verandahs. Operating between the two buildings, the three toiled tirelessly.

The hostel was completed on Friday the 5th of February 1959, and it opened with an official ceremony two days later. Dad paid his builders wages and, being a no-fuss type of character, he headed out to Debesa without going to the opening, which happened to be his thirty-eighth birthday, 7th of February. Today, the CWA cottage remains but St Joseph's Hostel is gone, having succumbed to a fire many years ago.

As another busy year drew to a close, Dad worked full speed to have the house liveable for March the following year, when he would move his family there. My parents also made final arrangements to send Pepita south for schooling. It wasn't unusual for gudia to send their kids to boarding schools and Mum and Dad, together with Aggie and Tom, decided it was a wise move to do the same and send Pepita and Pat away. Moreover, they knew that if the two cousins were together, they would support each other and thus be less likely to miss home.

There was no senior high school in Derby so sixteen-year-old Cyril, an excellent student, was off to Aquinas College in Perth. Not wanting to let the opportunity pass, the parish ensured everyone knew he'd been at the Holy Rosary School since its opening. In the parish chronicle the following passage appeared: 'Junior results published, Cyril Puertollano passed with 6 subjects, the first coloured boy from Derby parish to pass Junior.' Airline bookings were made for the three to begin term one away. The girls would go to Stella Maris Presentation College in Geraldton. Pepita was nine and Pat thirteen when they climbed the steps of their MMA flight on the 9th of February 1959, heading to Geraldton. They were the first two Aboriginal girls to ever board at the all-girls' college.

For Mum and Dad, it was a load off their minds as they prepared to relocate to Debesa. Us younger kids' education, they would deal with later. It all depended on how profitable Debesa turned out to be.

CHAPTER 6

Debesa

Their rural idyll offered peace, tranquillity,
open spaces and a sense of belonging

He yanked the door firmly shut behind him, skipped down the three steps and crossed to the loaded Chev truck in the driveway. Relieved to have completed his Derby projects and to be heading to Debesa, Dad pulled the crank handle out from under the bonnet. He fitted it into the front of the vehicle and, with an almighty heave, turned the motor. It spluttered and groaned then settled into a steady rhythm.

Claiming a spot among the boxes of household goods, my brothers were chuffed to be travelling in the back of the truck with their adult Galician cousins. The bulk of our gear had already been moved to Debesa. I snuggled up to Mum on the front seat where I could snooze with my head on her lap, against her soft tummy and my little legs stretched out across Dad's lap. 'We'll have some sorting out to do when we get home,' he smiled at her.

We made two stops before leaving town. First, at the State Housing Commission office. 'All the best with the sheep, Frank,' the clerk offered a friendly handshake as he accepted the keys to the Stanley Street house. Dad then drove slowly down the potholed street to the Catholic presbytery.

It was the 19th of March 1959, the feast-day of St Joseph, when he collected his final payment from Father Kearney for the hostel. Standing outside the church after mass, the priest chuckled as he waved us goodbye, 'I'll call in on my next station round, have the altar ready.'

Yeeda Station was the next stop, where Dad collected two lengths of 6-inch bone casing for Tom Egan the driller, who was down to 155 feet on another bore at Debesa. This windmill, Dad would call Phillips. Travelling at 40 miles an hour, a journey that usually took about two hours from Derby took three. Given the recent rains, it was a slow and steady trip over a sloppy road. The clear, fresh water trapped in the hollows along either side of the road beckoned, but no-one wanted to stop to loll in its coolness. We all wanted to get home.

The Chev's engine hissed as Dad brought it to a standstill under a large boab tree next to the evolving homestead. Wiping sweat from our foreheads, our necks already smeared with dirt, we tumbled from the vehicle into a small construction site. Nestled tidily alongside a pile of river sand and stones was a cement mixer and two upended wheelbarrows. Under a large, beige canvas, an assortment of long and short handled shovels, trowels and carpenter's tools rested.

Joe and Julio helped Dad unload the truck as Franky and Phillip disappeared into the lofty branches of the boab tree. Later, I sat with Mum on the doorstep. 'How do you spell my name?'

With feet buried in soft pindan, I looked up at her as she

smiled down at me – 'J-a-c-i-n-t-a,' the phonics softly rolling off her tongue. She then picked up a stick and drew my name in the damp earth. I took it from her and traced the letters.

As I grew older, there were more questions. 'Who are we Mummy?'

'Nigena. We're Nigena people,' she would tell me, 'from this side,' as she waved her arm in a wide arc towards Liveringa. 'Close up along the river, right up to Derby. Granny and Grampa, too, before they was taken away to Beagle Bay and Drysdale.' A deep frown crossed her forehead. It was something she only ever talked about with her siblings and mission folk. She knew who her ancestors were, where her parents had come from and who took them away. Her parents had made sure of that. I never understood fully nor ever questioned why my grandparents were taken from their mothers until I took up Aboriginal studies at university in the late 1980s. By then, I was already in my late thirties. What a confronting revelation that was, learning about racist policies that determined Aboriginal people's lives well into the future. But it was our Spanish heritage that dominated who we were – even though we lived in the Nigena bush. Perhaps being Spanish was more intriguing. In reality, it was the way white Australia would have us think about ourselves.

For two days my cousins helped Dad prepare for shearing before he took them across to Camballin to work in the rice fields for Kim Durack. He hoped they would be okay, remembering his own experiences of being taunted because of his imperfect English. But deep down he knew they would be all right.

Momentum picked up after my parents moved to Debesa. It was an exciting time for them even if, as small landowners, they were essentially alone. Both were hard workers and comfortable in their chosen way of life. I wonder now if they even imagined the steep learning curve they were in for, running a remote station while raising four young children. Living on a small, isolated property with parents who were strict Catholics meant that us kids had a sheltered upbringing that would affect our ability to socialise easily in the long run. We were innocent, humble kids with strong moral values nurtured in a religious environment. Moreover, we were a contented lot. Innocent of the world at large while in the company of our beloved parents and close relatives. Life was good.

My parents' contribution to pastoralism was shaped by their commitment as a married couple. There was no interference from outsiders and their division of labour was balanced. They were a team. They found the energy and determination to face new challenges. It was an arduous slog in trying climatic conditions where Mum did men's work and Dad did women's. Weaving divisions of labour into a tapestry of blended support for one another, they imagined an enduring future. Optimism and God were central to their very existence.

Mum was a stoic matriarch in whom Dad had found his equal. Like the 'mixed-descent' Aboriginal wives of other gudia station owners, Frank Lacy at Mount Elizabeth and Fred Russ at Gibb River in the northwest Kimberley, Mum was his right-hand woman. Her, Teresa Lacy's and Laura (Booty) Russ's contribution to pastoralism was different to the way in which white pastoralists relied on, and used, 'full-descent' women. In the East

Kimberley and the Northern Territory earlier in the century, for instance, Aboriginal women worked with stock and they partook in men's traditional roles. My mother's contribution to the pastoral industry, however, was based on a very different set of circumstances. She was mission raised. Refined in domestic skills, she had been trained to be subservient to gudia.

Katie with her children 1957
© Frank Rodriguez, photographer

Mum now sported a more mature, well-rounded figure. Her long, dark hair worn in a bun glittered with silver strands, and her stern face, in part due to the stroke, suggested a forthright individual. Yet under the facade was a warm, thoughtful person who others knew they could talk over their problems with. Despite the onset of type 2 diabetes, my mother was resilient and resourceful and a crucial part of Debesa's progress. Dad, on the other hand, might have been an introvert but he was well equipped with the necessary traits of 'brawn, courage, toughness and durability' (as Ann McGrath lists in her book, *Born in the Cattle*) to run a station. He relied on Mum to help with stock, run fences, load trucks and pull windmills.

Her role in helping Dad do the heavy lifting may well have added to her health problems given that Mum had two miscarriages during this time. Alone on the station with their children, I can only imagine how they must have dealt with those deeply traumatic and distressing times. All I ever knew was that I had two more brothers who never survived.

Dad was an incessantly busy small landowner who Horrie Miller respected because, unlike himself, Frank Rodriguez was an adept hands-on manager. Mr Miller's contribution came in the form of sourcing machinery and other equipment, though not always in ways that were helpful. The Land Rovers and machinery he bought were second-hand and run-down, which only added to the challenges Dad was already dealing with in his role as the manager. Once, when Dad was in urgent need of a tractor tyre, Mr Miller delivered a spare in his small Wackett aeroplane. As the noisy aircraft flew low over the trees towards the homestead, Mum quickly rushed Phillip inside for fear he would be hit by an airborne tyre. My young brother watched in awe as the tyre, like a mosquito escaping its predator, dropped from the plane. It hit the ground 'running' and disappeared into the bush.

Mr Miller often visited Debesa unannounced given there was no way of communicating. If Mary Durack was in Broome, she would make sure he had food for the trip, snacks that were inevitably unpalatable by the time he arrived. His drinking water in a sherry bottle was hot, lying on the front seat wedged alongside a packet of melted Devon Cream biscuits that were covered with ants. His Land Rover could be heard churning its way through the scrub well before it appeared at the homestead. For some reason, he only ever drove in via a seldom-used sandy track. 'Mister Miller's here,' someone would holler. Sometimes one of his six children was with him. Marie Rose, his youngest daughter and a year older than Pepita, got along well with my sister. Marie chatted to me about those times – how she joined in saying the rosary under the clearest, brightest night sky then listened to my parents talking softly after we were supposed to be asleep. Lying in bed quietly, she crushed tomato leaves between her fingers and inhaled the sweet, subtle smell as she watched embers in the wood stove fade into the night. Marie liked my mother's cooking too, smothering her lamb chops with Mum's delectable tomato relish. She had fun scuffling with the boys on the lawns, swimming in the tanks, laughing at the frogs in the toilet and climbing our boab tree. The sole cashew tree was even bigger than the one at her home in Broome and she was in awe of the way Dad humanely euthanised a sheep with a cancerous growth on its head. Mr Miller's time was usually spent tinkering with the motor of a Land Rover, the tractor or the bulldozer. He only ever stayed a night or two then was gone again.

In the same vein that Dad came to respect the advice of his stockmen during mustering time, Horrie Miller trusted Dad's judgement about road, windmill and dam placements. Together they mapped windmill sites, usually in a paddock corner. Mr Miller must have been quite pleased that some mills were named after his family too. Robins and Julies, after two of his daughters, were already pumping away when Dad named a swamp in the paddock closest to Derby 'Marie Soaks'. Later, he named three more mills for the family – Millers, Marys and Johnsons. A favourite mare was called Patsy, but I was never sure whether she was named after the eldest Miller or whether the horse came with the name. A frisky horse, Patsy threw Frenny Djinga on one muster. Frenny, who often worked at Debesa, suffered a bad cut to his head that left him in the Derby hospital for a few days. Andy Miller, like my brother Franky, never had anything named after him.

Johnsons Mill, 1960s © Frank Rodriguez, photographer

Shearing time was upon them again and Dad sought stock-men from nearby stations and from town. Usually it was our countrimin who came and stayed for the short season. Frenny came across from Liveringa while Sammy and his wife, Maisy, who helped Mum, came out from Derby with their small daughter. The men and Dad heaved six bales of wool onto the truck, securing them with ropes. 'I should be home for supper,' he called to Mum as he set off for Derby with the first wool of the season. We always called teatime 'supper'. He delivered the small, yet important, consignment straight to the Derby woolshed.

Duncan Beaton happened to be in from Noonkanbah furnishing the CWA cottage. The staging house had cost more to build than anticipated due to a shortage of building mate-rials and because of the alterations that Beaton had demanded Mr Miller agreed to accept the outstanding payment with 750 ewes. He was concerned that Beaton expected Dad to make the alterations at Debesa's expense, as he told Cyril Gare, 'This will be the last deal of a nature like this, I hope. However, this is the way the big stations get their work done, on the cheap.'

With shearing over, Dad asked Sammy and Frenny for the best route to muster the ewes across from Noonkanbah. They knew the country well. Dad admired their knowledge of the land, its layout and where, culturally, they could and could not cross. Both had spent long days mustering and camping at watering holes and windmill sites with Grampa during Liveringa musters. Dad benefited from such occasions and learnt, unaware that his stockmen's 60,000-plus years of heritage had empowered them to give the best advice.

At Noonkanbah no sheep were ready. Beaton said he needed another day to bring them in so Dad decided to visit Quanbun, 48 kilometres away, in the hope that Jeff Rose had sheep to sell. Perhaps, too, Rose could spare a stockman for the muster. 'Sorry Frank. No sheep and my stockmen are busy,' Rose scoffed.

Over the next six days Sammy and Frenny pushed the large flock towards Debesa. Past Sandy Billabong to Broken Wagon camp and beyond to Mount Wynne, bringing them halfway to Debesa where Dad met the muster with an extra stockman and horse. So far, all was going well. As the Mardoowarra floodplains became distant and the flock moved through the Erskine Ranges towards the Debesa boundary, Frenny sensed Dad's concern. He reassured him, 'Big mob water everywhere with fresh grass, Brank. Plenty tucker for sheeb.' Given that the stockmen knew the landscape well, it was no surprise the eleven-day journey went without a hitch. This was different to Dad's earlier experience when his truck became bogged and he had to wait a day until the muddy track dried out. He could smile now. A gratified smile. Debesa was progressing well so he took Sammy and his family to Derby for a break and he dropped Frenny back at the Liveringa camp. Nigena Lore time was looming and Frenny would be absorbed on 'walkabout' business for a few days. Dad respected the way in which he and other stockmen paid homage to their beliefs. A few days later he returned to pick him up, along with an extra stockman.

In mid-May, Phillip developed a swollen mouth. Mum was worried so she gathered us three kids and had Dad take us to town. After my brother was cleared by the doctor, we stayed on in Derby with Aggie while Dad returned to Debesa with Franky. At only seven years of age my older brother was learning to be a level-headed stockman with a strong work ethic. They returned a couple of days later in time to meet Pepita and Pat, home for the school holidays.

Excitement bubbled the day MMA's DC-3 touched down at the Derby airport. Our big sister was home from down south. Three and a half months was the longest any of us had ever been apart. We had all missed her and we hung off every word she said about boarding school and her new friends. The huge college on a hill had polished wooden stairs inside the front door that seemed to go up forever to her dormitory. She shared the dorm with several other girls who came mostly from the Geraldton district, but some did come from the northwest and the Kimberley. The town itself was a port from where the region's farmers shipped their grain, while offshore at the Abrolhos Islands a crayfish (rock lobster) industry was well underway. The boarders even went swimming in the ocean, something we could never do in Derby, being nestled on a peninsula surrounded by mudflats. We all looked up to my older sister. As my parents' first surviving child, Pepita was a favourite. Moreover, as the eldest, Pete, as the family came to call her, was a great help to Mum, especially given my mother's declining health.

Before heading home, Dad picked up the station's stock and mail. With us all in the Land Rover, he made a special detour downtown to Aylings store to collect his brand-new Sportmatic rifle. He couldn't wait to try it out. Nearing the homestead, he pulled over as we all looked on in awe. 'Shoo now, be quiet,' Mum said softly as Dad aimed at the stationary kangaroo almost hidden in the shadows of the scrub. With one accurate shot he downed the 'roo, which was then heaved onto the back of the Land Rover and taken home for supper. My Dad had become proficient with a gun. He already had a shotgun and a 303 rifle – essential trappings for station life.

With the earth still soft he continued making roads through the scrub, where the hard-to-conquer wattle became the bane of his existence. Nonetheless, he persisted in clearing it to make roads by towing a triangular shaped fire-plough made from heavy iron girders behind a tractor.

That year, everyone thought the wet was over when the weather suddenly changed and strong winds from the southeast buffeted the small station, continuing to do so in the coming days. A nameless cyclone was forming south of Wyndham as Dad prayed for more rain. His prayers were answered as unseasonal rains fell at the end of May 1959, nourishing the West Kimberley and making road construction easier for the time being. For the first time since the early 1900s a cyclone was given a name. It was called Betsy.

In Mr Miller's absence Dad ran the station doing burn-offs, fencing and assembling windmills with the help of Grampa or a station hand, but more often than not it was Mum by his side. Ongoing upgrades and construction work on nearby properties lured him away. My folks needed the money. At Liveringa he worked on the top house for Kim Rose and at Camballin he cemented the sloping walls of a public swimming pool that was being constructed for the Northern Development Company.

———

Debesa homestead, 1960s © Frank Rodriguez, photographer

Dad fast-tracked the Debesa homestead. The foundations he had laid in 1956 were slowly turning into a functional home. The floors stretched out for 3 metres from the centre room and walls of corrugated iron surrounded the open-plan house. He expanded the kitchen and added a dining room and three bedrooms. The house was effectively a closed-in verandah. Cut into the corrugated-iron walls he fashioned large push-out shutters, each with a strong timber slat to hold it open. Skilful on her Singer treadly, Mum prettied the open windows with lightweight gingham that fluttered in the occasional breeze. But they were no deterrent to insects invading the house, nor the odd bird that found itself caught below the hot tin roof. This was how we came to have Polly, our much-loved rainbow lorikeet. Polly the parrot adopted us.

Flying in through a window at mealtimes to peck from our plates, 'She's eating my food,' I'd cry.

'Well you're not eating it,' Mum chided me as she picked up a fork to force-feed me. I was a terrible eater. My brothers even called me Widge – a name that stuck for many years, to my loathing. Once satisfied, Polly balanced herself on the back of a chair or on Phillip's shoulder. He would walk around the yard with her perched there. She disappeared one day but sometime later, to our delight, reappeared with her babies. We watched as they hopped around in the branches of a poinciana tree, chirping and screeching. Then they were gone. We never saw Polly again.

Phillip with Polly, 1962 © Frank Rodriguez, photographer

My folks were wonderful improvisers. Cupboards were fashioned from timber crates and fronted with colourful materials. To the walls in the girls' bedroom Dad fitted shelving that he painted white. Great pride was taken as we placed the neatly folded linen and clothes in their rightful place on the shelves. In the boys' room the shelves were soon filled with toys – trucks, soldiers, guns, shanghais, boab nuts, marbles, pebbles and comics – leaving little room for clothing.

A combined laundry and bathroom was attached to the house, complete with cement wash troughs and a shower. 'What's that for Daddy?' I asked him, pointing to a small brandy bottle in the shower caddy.

'It's special ointment to stop my hair from falling out,' he said as he tapped his receding hairline. The concoction of brandy and aftershave lotion that he rubbed into his scalp may well have had the desired effect. Dad always had thin hair, yet he never went bald.

In the dry season, willy-willies seemed to appear out of thin air. Like tiny tornados, their red dust gathered sticks and leaves before slamming into the side of the house, bleeding pindan down the outer walls. When a bigger event occurred later in the year, a dust storm, it billowed in across the paddock – a tsunami of red dirt enveloping the house.

As kids we didn't seem to notice the oppressive heat that came with the 'build-up' to and during the wet. In an attempt to counteract its intensity, Mum hung a dripping wet blanket in a doorway to catch any breeze, which only slightly cooled the inside. Within minutes, the blanket was bone dry. Facing east across the home paddock, huge dark clouds rolled towards us in the late summer afternoons, which my parents surely prayed would deliver cooling rains. But mostly there was nothing. Dark shrouds of rain could be seen stretching to the horizon, greening the landscape elsewhere, but the clouds failed to reach the homestead. They thinned out before completely evaporating, only to reappear the next afternoon. 'Just teasing us,' we would sigh.

When an electrical thunderstorm did flash lightning, thunder cracked overhead and heavy raindrops splattered on the roof, we quickly drew the shutters in. The house plunged into darkness as the rain intensified – the pelting on the roof deafening. As the storm dissipated the noise segued into a happy yet disharmonising sound of croaking frogs in their element. An irritating sound unless you had a liking for frogs, which I did. Hail, the size of thumb balls (marbles), littered the lawns while the refreshing aroma of soaked vegetation hung in the air.

As the heat increased and the wet set in, my folks looked to the night sky, 'See that hazy ring around the moon? That means a cyclone is forming.' Then, true to the hazy ring indicator, any atmospheric low-pressure system forming off the coast was a sure sign a cyclone was brewing, with promises of decent rains.

Gardening, for my parents, was a necessary yet enjoyable pastime. Both were green-fingered and they welcomed the distraction from more tedious tasks. It's little wonder they took to gardening with ease, given their respective backgrounds – Dad growing up in rural Spain and Mum on a mission run by Europeans. Community gardening was part of their psyche. It didn't take long for the couch lawn to spread its tentacles around the house, and around vincas, oleanders, frangipani, bougainvillea and hibiscus. Poinciana, mango and lemon trees took centre stage while a lone cashew tree, the one that Marie remembered, grew near the lawn's edge. Hardy buxus blue-bell hedges sprouted along the fence. We chewed on the small, sweet flower bulbs. Nourished with compost and topped with mulch and sheep's manure, my folks' gardens flourished.

They didn't master a few species, though, like the orange tree.

It never grew very high and only produced dry, tasteless green fruit. As for the grapevine, it just didn't survive. If Dad had any ideas of making his own wine, like the families in Galicia, he was disappointed. He became excited when the spindly vine growing in a cool spot next to a dripping tap outside the bathroom produced a couple of tiny grapes. But they soon withered and died, as did any thoughts of a viticulture venture at Debesa.

On the western side of the house, few plants survived the hot afternoon sun. Vegetables, on the other hand, did very well in their designated plots. Every year a garden was prepared in a different place to let the previous year's soil regenerate. Thriving on Debesa's generous water supply, like a healthy European market garden, runner beans climbed the chicken mesh alongside sprouting corn, eggplants, carrots, Chinese cabbages, apple cucumbers and rockmelons. The Main Roads camp nearby on the Great Northern Highway bought the Debesa produce, while my folks sold tomatoes and watermelons to shops in town. 'Look at the size of this tomato, would you? It weighs a pound!' Pat, the counter lady at Elders, squealed as she held up the large red specimen to the grins of her customers and my proud parents.

Next to the house, Dad had built a bough shed with spinifex roof. Mum planted a Mexican creeper alongside that blossomed pretty little pink flowers. Some called it 'bride's tears' or 'hearts on a chain'. It survives today despite the bough shed being long gone. We often had meals there and it is where we celebrated Christmas. With us kids sleeping in the back of the Land Rover and Mum snoozing in the passenger's seat, Dad would drive through the night back to the station after midnight mass in Derby.

Beyond the bough shed stood our improvised cubby house – a boab tree. The very one that Franky and Phillip had disappeared into the day we moved to Debesa. It belonged to the family of trees that once played significant roles in northern Indigenous cultures. Boab trees provided food, water storage, medicines and raw materials to make rope, cloth, twine and boats. They gave shelter to women giving birth and they provided religious sites and were even used for entombment. Unlike the stand-alone potbelly prison boab at Myalls Bore (previously Mayalls Well) with its gaping 'door', our tree grew in three sections.

Standing upright, the main trunk's chubby girth measured 6 metres while slender, leafy antennae stretched 15 metres into the sky. My brothers nailed dog spikes into its girth so they could climb to the highest branches and with tomahawks they chopped steps into the well-proportioned arm that jutted to the right. We loved that tree. It meant something to each of us. For me, the third and narrowest limb stretched parallel to the ground at a perfect height for a small child to use as a kitchen bench. There, I made mud cakes and sucked on the pulp of boab nuts soaked in sweetened water, spitting out the seeds. 'You'll get belly ache from that stuff,' Dad warned. But we never did.

Living under the tree was a carpet snake that Dad chose not to alert us to. Absorbed in our childhood gratifications, we were oblivious to its presence until it came out to die. At any rate, and armed with a lot of respect mind you, we became used to snakes around the place – especially king browns. 'I remember that! I can remember snakes being in your house,' my cousin Shirley laughed.

Our boab tree, 2003 © Cindy Solonec, photographer

Debesa's buildings stood close to one another and they were all made of the same standard cement floors, jarrah pillars, corrugated iron and asbestos walls. The homestead was the first building, with a four-berth men's quarters where Mr Miller and the shearers camped a few yards away. Mum always ensured that fresh linen was on the beds whenever anyone stayed there. Behind stood a combined workshop and garage, while the blackfullas' camp was furthest from the homestead. Intended as a temporary base for casual workers, their hut had a kitchen with wood stove, sleeping area separated by jarrah planks with no wall panelling – a job that Dad intended to complete in due course – and three or four camp beds with straw mattresses and pillows. There was an outdoor ablution block and a bough shed, where people preferred to sleep, with their swags spread on the ground.

'What you cooking? Can I have some?' I asked Amy as I whiffed the delicious aromas of kangaroo stew. She was old Jerry's wife. With their adult daughter Aggie, they sometimes came across from Willumbah when Dad needed help in the off-mustering season. They were related to us but, like most of our full-descent relatives, I never did learn the exact connections. Sitting on the ground I cuddled up to Amy as she stirred the camp oven nestled on hot coals.

'Ngi (yes). Kungaroo, you can have 'em, and damper,' she offered as she chewed contentedly on her moolijin (tobacco rolled in eucalyptus ash). Granny also loved to chew on her moolijin, which she kept in a tobacco tin. The campfire played host to a gurgling billy placed on the embers. The stove inside was rarely used. My brothers and I liked being in the camp – lying on the beds and reading comics while listening to Slim Dusty, Jim Reeves, Buddy Williams and other country singers. It was from the stockmen that my brothers learned to play the guitar.

As a child I had a well-functioning, vibrant imagination stimulated by fairytales. For a birthday Mum had given me a book of fairytales that I loved. I can still see that book with its red cover with Little Red Riding Hood and a sneering wolf. Boab trees I imagined to be secret princess's hideaways with all the fairytale trimmings and beautiful, glittering tulle and chiffon floral dresses and satin shoes. I imagined myself to be like Cinderella, perhaps because her name was similar to my own. Alas, I was alone with no-one to share my imaginings. My sister had outgrown playing dolls, so I indulged in Matchbox cars with Phillip. We built roads around the side of the house between the bedroom and the bough shed and through Mum's vinca flowerbeds.

One day as we played with our trucks, our clothes and little faces covered in dirt, we became aware of movement in the bush, close to Mr Miller's track. A dark mass slowly emerged from the scrub, coming towards the house. Our imagination got the better of us as we ran crying to Mum, 'Yow mummy, something there in the bush, coming here, look,' as we pointed to the now clear figures walking towards the house.

'Don't be stupid. What's wrong with you two? That's Aunty Maggie and Uncle Rodney,' she laughed. Uncle Rodney was Grampa's brother, and they always stayed close to us. With them was a young stockman from Lulugui Station. The three had been dropped off at the mailbox and they'd walked in to visit. They stayed at Debesa until Dad would take another store run to town. Mum always enjoyed having Aunty Maggie at Debesa. She filled the emptiness Mum felt being away from her sisters.

Shearing sheds are great places for kids and Debesa's was no different. In a classic northwest style, it was set 200 yards from the homestead. Its tree-trunk pillars supported the spinifex ceiling and corrugated-iron roof with an occasional wall to protect the shearing equipment and the wool from the elements. Helping round up the sheep while taking in the smells of lanolin and manure mingled with pindan and bush foliage was shearing time. 'Hey, you kids, push those blasted sheep through the gate into the yard. Get Raphael in front,' a frustrated Dad yelled as the sheep darted off in the wrong direction. It wasn't unusual for him to lose his cool and swear in Spanish so that we didn't learn to cuss. Merinos are notoriously dumb, following each other around and around in circles until one leads the way forwards, or backwards. Our pet ewe, Raphael, became an accidental helper. Lured with a Weet-Bix or slice of bread, she ran towards us standing at the far end of the yard with the whole flock hot on her hooves, through the narrow gate right to where Dad wanted them.

Phillip and Cindy, Debesa, 1960 © Frank Rodriguez, photographer

The wonderful thing about Debesa is that we had a lot of pets. Even feral cats that Dad neutered became our pets. But generally it was orphaned lambs or joeys found alongside their dead mothers and brought into the homestead that boosted our menagerie.

It's how Raphael and Rusty came to be with us. Family friend Raphael Dolby was travelling from Fitzroy Crossing to Derby when he came across a ewe that had been hit by a vehicle, her newborn waiting by her side. Knowing that Debesa was further up the road, he brought the female lamb in and she was duly named after him. Raphael remained with us for many years as a favourite pet. Walking into the house, clip-clopping across the cement floor and 'baaing' with lamb in tow, 'What you got? Another baby Raphael,' Mum would welcome her.

Tailing time at Debesa was always busy and a bonus when it coincided with the school holidays. We learned to flip a lamb onto its back, grasp its legs tightly then heave it onto the tailing bench. Holding it as firmly as we possibly could, Dad quickly pierced the ear with the Debesa earmark, then swiftly severed the tail with a very sharp tailing knife. Daubing the wounds with a kerosene-soaked rag, he released the lamb to run off bleating into the flock, searching for its mother. Selected male lambs he neutered with rubber bands. Using an elastrator to stretch a rubber band, he snapped it around the base of the lamb's scrotum, which would eventually shrivel up and drop off. At the end of the day, the pile of lambs' tails was dug into hot coals, hangi style. When cooked, we peeled the wool away from the flesh and seasoned with salt. Lamb tails tasted divine.

Dad was close to nature. Not just with his gardening ability and how he could predict the weather based on the antics of birds and insects, but also in the way he disposed of animals, which was nothing short of humane. He did what had to be done. Feral kittens he removed from the shearing shed roof, injured animals like emus half strangled in a fence, aged or sick sheep, and pink joeys found in a dead mother's pouch, he euthanised discreetly.

Fully developed joeys he brought home. From their improvised pouch that was a hessian rice bag hanging low on a wall in the storeroom, they tumbled in and out to follow us around the house and the yard. When mature enough, they disappeared into the bush. Occasionally a doe returned to introduce her young. Kangaroos are matriarchal, which is probably why she returned to her human family. 'Look who's over there,' Mum calmly pouted her lips towards the bush. Lilly sat quietly under a gum tree with joey peering from her pouch.

As she lingered in the shadows an owl perched above, camouflaged by the tree as though guarding the kangaroos. I often saw owls sitting in the trees, motionless, staring through tunnel vision. I wondered if they were even alive, they sat so still. Mum always said to leave them be, they couldn't see during the day. Many years later, I learned from my daughters that our totem was the owl. On a journey of discovery, always keen to know about their Nigena heritage, they had asked their own wise guru, Nanna Leena, what their totem was. The younger generations are keen to learn more about their Indigenous heritages these days. No longer are they told that Aboriginal beliefs and languages are rubbish and not to be bothered with them. We never harmed or even ate owl, as we did other species of birds. Now I know why.

Franky and Phillip, Debesa, 1964
© Frank Rodriguez, photographer

Our parents ensured that we weren't indifferent to our Nigena and Galician heritages. Regardless of the overriding thrust by governments that all Australians would eventually live an Anglo-Australian way of life, our parents continued to embrace their respective cultures. Yet, like our mother, we were being grounded in English and Catholicism. Living on country nonetheless meant that we were not totally denied the chance to learn about bush life. We took our existence for granted.

Knowing what was in the bush pantry and how to collect and eat ngili-ngili, nalgut, kungerberries and sugarbag was par for the course. Magabala was my least favourite fruit. I found it difficult to eat with its hairy tresses around the tasty section, and I always managed to chomp into the bitter part.

We spoke local Kriol and Aboriginal English, though learning to speak Nigena or Spanish escaped us. We only ever learned a few words. 'How do you say butter in Spanish, Daddy?' one of us would ask as we sat around the table.

'Mantequilla,' he'd reply, pleased we were taking an interest in his language.

'Pass the mantequilla ... hang on, how do you say "please" in Spanish?'

'Por favor. But you don't need to say please.' In time I would come to realise how proper, how snooty the English can be. So it came to pass that we knew most items on the table in Spanish – pan (bread), azúcar (sugar), agua (water), leche (milk) – and we learned courtesies – 'buenos dias' (g'day) and 'adios' (goodbye). At bedtime our parents would call, 'buenos noches' (good night). It was tough for Dad with his family not being immersed in his culture, especially when he was the only speaker. We never took him seriously. Teaching Franky, the hyperactive wit of the family, to say 'gracias' (thank you) was a waste of time because it always ended with us in chortles as he deliberately enunciated 'grassy arse'.

Our home might have been minimalist, but it was comfortable. Open-plan living did lend itself to making housework easier. With straw broom in hand, Mum steered the dust right back out the door. Her work was never-ending and it didn't go unnoticed by my cousins Pat and Shirley, who sometimes stayed at Debesa. Pat liked being by her side when us younger ones were off playing. She helped Mum and she learned from her, 'Your mother was always there for me.' Shirley added, 'Your mother was quite spritely you know, in those early days before she got her diabetes. Your mother was as strong as a lion. Full on. She used to work, work and work. I remember her doing the washing all the time in Debesa, by hand. A large pile of clothes on washing day, not just a little bit of clothes.'

In the kitchen, between the stove and the sink, stood a treasured large blue table that Dad had made. It is where food was prepared. Large shutters opened out from it over the lawn to view a pet lamb or joey grazing in the late afternoon and chooks pecking in the grass. Beyond the lawn was a wire clothes line, held up with wooden stakes, and beyond that the wood heap. Dad was not impartial to domestic chores and he enjoyed cooking. Proud of his ancestry, he took delight in showing Mum how to make tortilla, one of Spain's favourite dishes. But it was Mum who made the most delectable bread. Working at the blue table she kneaded and rolled out generous batches of dough, slicing off small pieces for Phillip and me to mould into shapes.

When baked, she tossed the loaves from their tins along with our creations onto the floured table. She smiled as she guardedly watched our little fingers find their way in to gouge a small hole in the end of a warm, fresh loaf. Mum cooked meals every day over a stifling Metters wood-fired stove. Mutton, our primary meat source, she turned into scrumptious dishes – roasts, stews, curries and burnt chops. Despite the heat, she even prepared jelly, adding canned fruits, and she made vanilla ice-cream from tinned evaporative milk, letting them set in the kerosene freezer.

Dad regularly shot a wether. Loading it onto the back of a Land Rover, he parked the vehicle under the gum tree near the fowl yard and hoisted it up by the back legs to hang just a metre off the ground. Out came the butcher knives and steel. The sound of blades sharpening was music to the ears of our cats, running from their slumber to feast on entrails and blood dripping to the ground. Nothing was wasted. The gut, heart, kidneys, liver, tripe and brains. Sheep's brains were tasty. Mum dipped the delicacy in egg and seasoned flour and deep-fried them. Franky wasn't even a teenager when he became proficient in skinning and gutting animals. In the same way that Pepita was relied on to help Mum with us younger ones, Dad was teaching Franky to do men's work from a very early age.

Beef was prized meat. Heaven help the beast that wandered onto Debesa property, taking down fences in the process. Phillips mill on the boundary was closest to cattle stations on the northern side of the property and occasionally a bullock that came to feed on juicy grasses and drink from the troughs became the target of my Dad's 303 rifle. The downed bullock, too big to transport in the Land Rover, was butchered on site and the choice cuts taken home. Bush ducks and bush turkey often graced our table, while pigeons and barnies (racehorse goanna) were tossed onto the campfire during mustering time. Mr Miller sometimes brought fresh fish from Broome that he gave to Mum tightly wrapped in newspaper. It was how he kept it cool on the long journey.

The workload for Mum increased at shearing time when a team of two shearers, a wool classer and shed hands stopped for smoko twice a day. Sandwiches or Sao biscuits spread with butter and jam or vegemite, or a slice of meat and pickles, were packed into a basket with beverages that us kids took down to the shearing shed. Phillip at just six years of age, when the rest of us were away at boarding school, managed on his own carrying a large teapot filled with piping hot tea. Making a beeline for the shearing shed, he didn't stumble nor lose a drop. Mum prepared meals for everyone. When Mr Miller was at Debesa, she was the perfect host – stepping up to impress him with her culinary skills.

In the kitchen opposite the blue table stood an open kitchenette filled with eating essentials, a set of turquoise dining and side plates, matching teacups with saucers, beakers and a few pannikins. Cutlery and cooking utensils cosied in a tea-towel-lined box sat on the bottom shelf. Alongside the kitchenette stood a 5 foot high, flywire-enclosed pantry cupboard filled with condiments – herbs, spices, plain and self-raising flours, yeast, powdered custard, jelly crystals and tins of Sunshine milk. Atop the pantry sat a battery-operated wireless. That radio was my father's vice.

He listened to the ABC News every night via shortwave. Generally, it was Radio Australia. With his ear pressed firmly to the wireless he incessantly fiddled the dial, trying to stay with the best reception. The evening's atmospheric conditions suited interference from Indonesian radio stations that crackled and surged over the national broadcaster. To make things worse for him, our closed-in verandah home was perfect for small children to play hidey in. After the evening meal, while the older siblings did the dishes, Phillip and I would run through the house and into the centre room, hiding between the two kerosene fridges and screaming when found. We drove Dad nuts as he tried to listen to the news above the already static reception.

The wireless was indeed a luxury. Mum enjoyed listening to the cricket – she only ever supported the Indian and Pakistani teams. 'I'm not barracking for England or Australia because Percy Rose didn't care about Grampa. Not like Nygumi. He looked after Granny and all of us.' Both my parents kept up to date with the tennis too since the Spaniard, Manolo Santana, was at the top of his game during the 1960s. *Blue Hills*, a soap opera that ran for twenty-seven years, was popular with country people. It was with little surprise then that Dad sometimes appeared for lunch just as the day's episode began at 12.30 pm. Coming through the open door and ducking into the bathroom all hot and sweaty, 'Has it started yet?' he called, then chomped on a salt tablet to rehydrate the bodily fluids he'd lost through perspiration. Curious about those tablets I nibbled on one and recall that it was extremely salty. I wondered how he could even chew on them.

Later, my folks would discuss the characters as though they were dear friends before he headed back to work servicing windmills, cleaning troughs, repairing a fence and checking on newborn lambs. The wireless kept us connected to the outside world. In later years, during school holidays us kids tuned in to the afternoon session of Perth ABC's *Yours for the Asking* to hear requests we had sent in for our boarding school friends, and vice versa.

Our house was lit solely by kerosene-fuelled tilly and hurricane lamps and burning embers in the wood stove. Early in the 1960s Mr Miller proudly brought a semblance of modernity to Debesa – a second-hand 12-volt power plant. It was a noisy, smelly, petrol-fuelled motor that sat outside the bathroom wall facing the kitchen in a cabinet that Dad built especially for the unit. A 'small powerhouse', he called it. Too small even to generate electricity for luxuries like fans. But Dad thought it was a bit of all right as he disclosed to his diary, 'All day about Debesa. H. Miller arrived here today with the batteries for the lights for the first time in Debesa. The little engine is running very well. Makes a bit of noise but otherwise is good.'

Times were a-changing as Dad fixed a power cable to the overhead planks and ran it through the house then secured a light globe to the dangling cable in each room. Light globes now adorned our house. Tugging the cord hanging next to the globe brought a bright light shining down. The light attracted swarms of flying ants and other insects so Dad strategically placed the globe away from the dining room table. Mum placed a large bowl of water on the floor directly under the light where, attracted to the reflection, insects kamikazed into the water. But when a light in another room was yanked on, each light became dimmer. They shone brightest when only one or two lights were on at a time. That meant the kerosene lamps and battery-powered torches were indispensable and remained as our reliable night-light sources for many years.

We often dragged our camp beds onto the lawn into the cool night air. Much better than sleeping in a house that had become so hot during the day from the sun beating onto the iron roof and walls. Pesky mosquitos were determined to make our outdoor sleep miserable. To foil them, our parents gathered and stoked kungerberry branches so the piquant scented smoke drifted around as a deterrent. To be extra sure we wouldn't be eaten alive, they rubbed our arms and legs with Dimp, a commonly used and effective liquid repellent with a very strong odour. In all likelihood, it was the foul smell that had more to do with the desired effect than the oil itself.

Every night we prayed. We sat on our beds saying the rosary and counting the five decades (ten Hail Marys) on our fingers, or on rosary beads if we were lucky to have a set. Cicadas joined in, chirping in the nearby foliage while the frogs' jolly cacophony resonated from near the wash house. For us kids, praying was tedious. Trying to outdo each other we raced through the rosary so quickly it became a mumbled chant. I wondered if Franky sometimes skipped a finger or two because he always finished counting to ten before I did. Interrupting the stillness of the night was the occasional soft pounding of a kangaroo that briefly unsettled nearby stock, while any writhing under a bed was a snake or lizard that sent us into giggles as we quickly drew our legs up.

Later, as we lay back cuddling our pets and peering into the night to spot slow-moving satellites amid the myriad of stars, the flickering light from a passenger jet could be seen heading west on its way to Singapore from Sydney. We became absorbed in the stories our parents told us about the galaxies. Pointing to and explaining the various formations in the glittering sky-show, we came to know the Milky Way, the Southern Cross, the Saucepan and the Seven Sisters. 'Mummy, tell us that story about the Seven Sisters again,' we pleaded. We listened intently while she retold the story as she knew it from growing up at Beagle Bay. Squinting into the cluster of stars I tried and tried to count the seven sisters until eventually I would fall asleep, having only ever seen five, unlike my siblings who claimed to see all seven.

My friend Munya Andrews was so inspired by the times she spent as a child in the 1960s exploring the brilliant cosmos spectacle that she wrote a book about it. In astronomy, the Seven Sisters are the cluster of stars known as the Pleiades, so she titled her book *Seven Sisters of the Pleiades.* From her adoptive grandmother Candice Cox on Noonkanbah, she learned how Aboriginal people are connected to the seven sisters. '[W]e are the same *mob* as them Munya. We are the *same* people. We come from the same country,' Candice would tell her. Like Munya, I too could imagine a cousin from the cluster dropping down to visit us.

Given that the Debesa homestead was only one mile from the main road, visitors sometimes dropped in unexpectedly, bringing mail and stores. Impromptu visits lent themselves to social interaction. The bush telegraph worked well between neighbours as conversations about station life were cheerfully deliberated over a cup of tea. Usually, though, the mail was collected on a store run to Derby. Some time later Dad fashioned a roadside mailbox from a 44-gallon drum. He painted it white, rested it on four metal fence pickets with the flap door facing away from the main road then painted DEBESA in black along its side. Somehow, it brought a sense of officialdom to the small lease.

A regular visitor was our Uncle Tom Puertollano. He was the owner-driver of a tip-truck and he worked for the Main Roads Department. He was often camped nearby – either at the Camballin turnoff, opposite Debesa's, or further east in the Erskine Ranges. He, too, brought mail and stores and sometimes he stayed the night. My parents always enjoyed his company and his job suited our cousin Cyril. Home on school holidays, it gave Cyril the ideal opportunity to spend time with his father and to be out in the bush. In turn, Mum and Dad called on Tom when they delivered vegies to the camp. I loved the camps as we drove slowly through the rows of tents. My imagination never idle, to me it was like a small town. Tom may have been my mother's brother-in-law, but he was Dad's best mate so it was a good thing that he was nearby when Dad was bitten along the inner arm by a centipede that caused severe swelling. With urgency Mum had Franky, who was barely able to reach the pedals and could hardly see over the steering wheel, drive to the camp. Tom then rushed his delusional mate to the Derby hospital.

All of us kids learned to drive in a Land Rover from an early age, sitting on Dad's lap. When we did graduate to the driver's seat alone a few gates and fences inevitably came down. I remember him yelling at me to put the brake on as I approached a gate. Too late. The heavy gate that ended up V-shaped stopped me instead! Nevertheless, we all became competent drivers, a legacy of the freedom we enjoyed on Debesa.

Mum, on the other hand, was the ever-reluctant motorist. Only when Dad was desperate did she get behind the wheel. He tried teaching her to drive and the one time I can recall ever being there, she ordered us all out of the Land Rover, 'Go on you kids, walk ahead, way ahead, long way,' flapping with her hands anxiously for us to move. Hardly out of sight we stopped abruptly in our tracks, bemused by the sound of crunching gears reverberating through the bush as the vehicle kangaroo-hopped towards us – Dad in the passenger's seat looking horrified.

———

School holidays were over in February 1960 and Pepita and Pat were ready to return to Stella Maris when, as often happened during the wet, the Derby airport closed following 140 points of rain overnight. The MMA flight was still in Port Hedland, delayed because of inclement weather in the East Pilbara. Dad could be impatient. Always with the station on his mind, he wondered how long it would be before the airport opened again. How long would he have to stay in town? For two days he was restless, itching to leave. There were things that needed to be done. The shearing shed and shearing plant had to be readied for shearing. Mustering needed to be done. He went back to Debesa.

A week passed and as he looked westward towards Derby, he could see that the rain had eased. Perhaps the airport would reopen, so he returned. Sure enough, it had, and on the 18th of February the girls flew out to Geraldton, with Dad there to say goodbye. Now my parents needed to make decisions about us younger kids' schooling. While Phillip and I, at four and six, were considered too young they thought to give correspondence a go for Franky. A teacher called at Debesa to make the necessary arrangements but, realistically, homeschooling was out of the question. Mum would have been fine since she had taught kids at Beagle Bay, but with running a station and her increasing health problems it was impracticable. Besides, Franky spent most of his time with Dad out on the station run so little formal education even took place.

Franky turned nine in February 1960 and for the first time he went to school. A boarder at St Joseph's Hostel, which was under the management of Mr and Mrs Rykers, the children were driven each day to the Holy Rosary School in Mr Rykers' little box van. Franky went straight into Grade 2, skipping Grade 1, already two years behind his classmates. Nonetheless, he settled well into St Joseph's. He enjoyed being with other kids and my parents breathed a sigh of relief that their energetic and carefree son was happy. Moreover, they were thankful the eldest two children were away at school as they enthusiastically continued with the business of developing their lease. Yet Dad missed having Franky around so whenever he could he took him out to Debesa for the weekend.

It was approaching the August school holidays as I sat on a bed with Kerry in Aggie's house, listening to Mum and Aggie talking. Kerry was already at the Holy Rosary and I wanted to be there too. I became a little excited as we eavesdropped, giggling. The two sisters often bounced things off each other, and now they were talking about me. It was August and at seven years of age, I still hadn't been to school. 'How old is she Katie?'

'Seven.'

'Well she's old enough to go to school. You must ask the sisters.' Before I knew it, I found myself boarding at St Joseph's Hostel too. I started in Grade 1 for the last school term of 1960 and I made my first holy communion during that time. Clearly Dad considered it a special occasion as I stood under a mango tree and he took photos of me with his box camera.

Cindy Rodriguez, first holy communion, Derby, October 1960 © Frank Rodriguez, photographer

Towards the end of the year Franky became extremely sick with an undiagnosed illness. Mum and Dad were so concerned they took no chances and removed us both from the hostel before the school term finished. Earlier that year, children at the hostel had become sick with influenza or pneumonia, which is what probably influenced their decision. The following year Franky was sent to St Patricks (St Pats) Christian Brothers College in Geraldton.

———

Technology in its various forms was emerging in 1960s West Kimberley. Mr Miller purchased a second-hand pedal radio for Debesa that was charged from a large battery sitting on the floor under a table. Dad delighted in being able to send a telegram via the outpost radio operators in Derby, while listening in to the trials and tribulations around the West Kimberley from other pastoralists. Grampa, too, was getting in on the changing times when he asked Dad to install a self-starter in his utility. Both were chuffed when it worked just fine. We all piled into the Land Rover and followed Grampa back to Willumbah, just in case – then we continued onto Camballin for picture night.

But technology wasn't always performing as it should. Sometimes the pictures weren't on. Either the reel hadn't arrived or, such as on this occasion, the projector was crawling with flying ants. It was, after all, the height of the wet season when the insects were at their thickest and seeking dry places to nest. The designated projectionist had the job of cleaning out the projector. 'We'll have to have pictures next week kids, once I get this thing going again.'

A mile or so over the rickety bridge that crossed Uralla Creek from the Camballin town site, where I almost met my fate as a toddler, was Joe and Julio's workplace. It was a corrugated-iron shed on a hill that could be seen shimmering in the midday sun as we drove towards it. Their job was to bag the rice ready for sale. The harvest was dumped into silos from where it spilled onto a conveyor belt and poured into bags attached to the end of the belt. Dad called it the 'bagging mill'.

Mum didn't mind taking trips to Camballin. That way, she could visit her folks at Willumbah then get Dad to continue on to Liveringa to see Aunty Maggie and Uncle Rodney, who lived in the blackfullas' camp. She took clothes and food and other essentials for them to share. He parked the Land Rover near the camp and Aunty Maggie and Uncle Rodney walked across to greet them. Always happy to see Mum, Aunty Maggie had the widest, most infectious grin you would ever see. The two were very close. Happy to see us kids too, she would gently stroke our arms and place her spindly hand on our necks, grateful for anything that Mum gave them.

Ellen and Tony Ozies and their six kids still lived in a workers' cottage halfway up 'the hill'. Forever generous, Tony showed off the four ducks he had shot that morning, 'Here Frank. Take them home for you and Katie for supper.' He knew how much Dad enjoyed tasty bush ducks. In turn, my folks had never left Debesa without eggs, boxes of tomatoes and watermelons to share.

Katie and Frank's fortieth wedding anniversary with Ellen and Tony Ozies, Derby, 1986
© Dieter Solonec, photographer

A few weeks later in the quiet of night we were awakened by the sound of a motor grinding its way towards the homestead. What travellers would arrive at this time? It wasn't Mr Miller because the sound was coming from the main entry point. On an overcast and humid night, Father Peile's vehicle emerged from the darkness. He, Granny, Grampa and Kerry were sitting inside looking bewildered. My grandparents were on their way to Debesa when their vehicle broke down on the other side of the Erskine Ranges. Grampa was not well.

He had had an accident while fixing fencing wire a few days before. As he tightened the wire it snapped and both ends flung back, piercing his left hand. Gangrene had set in, extending to his elbow joint, with his arm now incapacitated. Grampa was in need of urgent medical attention. He planned to reach Debesa for Dad to get him to the hospital when his vehicle broke down. The inclement weather had made it difficult for him to drive and the rain became heavier as he tried to get the motor restarted. Together the family prayed for help. Suddenly, Father Peile's vehicle appeared over the rise. He was heading towards Fitzroy Crossing on his station rounds and now he backtracked to Debesa with his passengers from where Dad immediately took them to Derby.

The injury would cause Grampa problems until his death in 1967. His employer, the KPC, considered the accident serious enough for them to pay for his treatment and his airfare to a Perth hospital. Kim Rose considered him 'a longtime, loyal and dedicated employee' when he wrote to the KPC board, instructing them to care for Fred Fraser. He was one of a kind, and had special connections to the Rose family, Kim argued. It wasn't until early in May that Grampa could return to work after a long stay in the Derby hospital.

———

By the middle of March 1,800 sheep had been shorn and the 450 lambs were looking healthier by the day. The shearer's next job was at Noonkanbah and Duncan Beaton turned up, dead on time, to collect him. Dad breathed a sigh of relief that the weather had stayed fine for the shearing to be completed in the two weeks, so the shearer could leave for his next contract. Dad and the stockmen loaded ten bales of wool and a few good-sized watermelons onto the truck and went to town with Mum. The melons he sold to Aylings store for £4 then spent the money on more bags of cement that he bought from Harbour and Lights for £10.

They stayed until Easter Sunday then picnicked with the Puertollanos by the Mardoowarra before heading home. Trips to Debesa from town were rarely straightforward. Family gatherings at Cuttings, or more often than not at Langi Crossing, not far from the Yeeda homestead, were par for the course. At Langi a cement bridge crossed the river on the main road that connected Derby and Broome. A large canvas was spread on the ground and Mum unpacked the food and put the billy on while we climbed paperbark trees (melaleuca) and waded in the river. Like our grannies before us, we played in the bush and gathered fruit before indulging in tinned corn beef, bread and tea and the heavenly trotters that Mum had seasoned and poached beforehand. 'Your pig trotters, Aunty Katie,' Shirley would tell my Mum as she tucked in, 'are the best.'

The Debesa stocks continued to build and a consignment of 350 healthy ewes and eight rams arrived aboard the SS *Delemere* midyear. After arranging for their delivery to the station, Dad and Georgy Dann called on Jeff Rose at Quanbun – but still, no sheep for sale. So the pair headed to Fitzroy Crossing via Jubilee

Downs Station. Always adventurous, they enjoyed bush bashing and this time they managed to get lost. Finding themselves on the riverbank, unable to cross to the town site, they retreated then ran out of petrol not far from Ellendale Station. The manager gave them two gallons, enough to get home at 9.30 for a late supper.

Taking risks and being accident prone were part of my Dad's journey in life. Us kids and Mum often mused over the years, 'It's a wonder he even survived Debesa.' Some accidents were more serious than others, like the time he fell from the 15-foot tank behind the workshop, narrowly missing a metal picket. His back suffered yet he somehow managed to continue working. As I read through his diaries, he seems to have often injured a foot in one way or another. Fortunately, most foot injuries appeared minimal. Perhaps, too, because he was so active, his injuries had a better chance of healing. One entry reads, 'Half a day working on the fence. My foot is feeling very sore, must be some grass seed somewhere on it is swelled up near the small toes. Time will tell what the trouble is. The weather seems very unsettled, so it could be some more rain about.' The swollen foot became excruciatingly sore. There didn't seem to be any seed embedded, but rather, 'You appear to have tinea,' the doctor said, ordering him to rest and take a course of antibiotics for three days. My father's forced rest was a blessing in disguise. It meant that Mum could spend precious time with her sisters.

Phillip, too, didn't escape accidents. He was four when Dad placed him on a horse for a ride, but he slipped off the saddle headfirst and cracked his head on a rock. He suffered a deep cut between his eyes where the scar remains today, a reminder of his childhood Debesa.

It was late July when Joe came to the station with exciting news. 'I'm going home to Galicia to marry my sweetheart, Visita,' he announced, 'and we will live at Camballin. She is very keen to come here.' In no time, he was back from Spain. On a hot, sweltering day in November, he and Visita drove into Debesa bearing gifts from the family in Spain. To our curiosity and delight, and despite not speaking a word of English, Visita was a vivacious and immediately likeable woman. Christmas Day gave the rest of the family the perfect opportunity to meet her. With the Puertollanos and with Granny, Grampa and Kerry we picnicked by the river at Camballin. We were showing off our culture. Swimming, catching jarrambas, fishing and feasting on kangaroo that Dad had shot and gutted under a tree. Aggie and Visita, both gregarious women, hit it off immediately. They became great friends.

Debesa kids, 1959 © Frank Rodriguez, photographer

CHAPTER 7

Debesa kids

I was going with the big girls
to boarding school down south

Debesa was our home and my folks had plenty to be contented about. The small station in the middle of the West Kimberley was making steady progress. Decent falls in February of 1961 saw foliage shrug off its inertia to produce widespread new growth as infectious grins appeared on the faces of locals. That is what good rains can do to Kimberlites.

Home on school holidays we were expected to do our fair share of work, like clean out the fowl yard. It teemed with chooks, ducks and a couple of cute bantams oblivious to their names – Tilly and Jack. Our job was to feed them, collect the eggs, clean the coops and replenish with straw that Dad bought from Camballin. Forgetting that snakes lurked in the coops, the fowl-yard jobs were fun. We used litres of water to scour out the ducks' pond while soaking each other as squawking chooks escaped up into the safety of the gum trees the fowl yard was built around.

There are many memories of Debesa – our sanctuary. The layout evolved over the years and as children we had plenty to do. Some 30 yards across the paddock was the homestead's first water supply. It's where my folks and their toddlers stayed in a tent in the early days. Secure on a cement base under the wind-mill's frame now sat a diesel motor that Dad serviced regularly. The narrower tank perched on a 20-foot-high stand had a pipe attached that ran water to the lower, wider tank – our impro-vised swimming pool. It's where my cousin Mandy Ahmat from Darwin always reminds me that she learned to swim. In fact, we swam in tanks throughout the station.

Frank, Pepita and Phillip (in the water), Julies Mill, 1960s
© *Frank Rodriguez, photographer*

The excess water from our swimming pool flowed into the horses' troughs and into a small holding paddock used for shearing time. There, in the shade of a cluster of bloodwood bushes and a bauhinia tree, Dad cemented in a pond for the stock. It became a magnet for birds. William Williams, who had grown up at Beagle Bay with Mum, showed Franky and Andy Miller how to make a bird trap from wooden slats and chicken mesh to place over the pond. The idea was to make a little pocket money by selling the finches they trapped. But it was short-lived. Phillip and I set the birds free, which incensed the older boys.

Meanwhile, my parents wanted to ensure we were reasonably well educated so when a salesman called at the station selling encyclopedias, they subscribed. For £283 a brand-new set of Encyclopedia Britannica, complete with solid wooden shelving, graced the middle room of the homestead right next to Dad's desk. Curious, we often delved into its pages, discovering wonderful facts about our world – Dad especially.

———

It was the second year of the Rodriguez/Miller partnership and nine years since Dad had taken up the Backland Downs lease. He was the hard-working, hands-on manager while Horrie Miller, in conjunction with his Perth-based accountant, managed the finances.

The partners continued to source sheep locally, bought with currency or by bartering. Agriculture Department personnel were regular visitors to Debesa as they undertook research into the viability of growing introduced grasses in the region. As at the Camballin paddy fields, Dad was intrigued, watching their growth. Bulldozer drivers from the Main Roads Department were regulars too. They inadvertently made useful small dams as they extracted gravel for the main road that skirted the length of Debesa.

Over at Liveringa, the mighty Mardoowarra had been undergoing a transformation. The Public Works Department built a dam on Uralla Creek that became known as the Seventeen Mile Dam and a barrage with huge collapsible floodgates across the river, 16 kilometres from the emerging Camballin township. The barrage was designed to halt the natural flow of the river. During the dry season with the gates open the trapped waters gushed into irrigation channels that watered the rice crops, destroying hallowed Aboriginal sites in the process. The scheme captivated the local psyche. As Dad worked around the district, he and Grampa watched its progress and they admired the rice project that ultimately became a failed experiment at Camballin.

The end of the long school holidays loomed now and Franky, at ten years of age, was excited about going to St Patricks College. Having had to skip Year 1 and doing only part of Year 2, he would go straight into Year 3. Shirley was heading to Stella Maris with Pat and Pepita. She would join the Year 7 class. A week later, on 20 February 1961, I moved in with Aggie and Tom to reboot my schooling at the Holy Rosary School.

There were three school terms a year and generally we went home for the holidays. Term 1 zipped by that year and at the end of the May holidays, Dad loaded the luggage into the back of the Land Rover for Term 2. This time there was an extra case bound for Geraldton. Mine! Even though I was only seven, my parents knew that I would be looked after by my sister and cousins. They must have been quite sure, too, that college education was best for me. After all, boarders my age and younger were there, though most did come from farms in the Mid West region, which meant their parents could visit them. Excited and bewildered all at the same time, I found myself skipping alongside my big sister across the Derby tarmac to the waiting DC-3. I was going with the big girls to boarding school down south.

It was some job for Mum, preparing us all for college. Living on a station, mail order proved to be the best way to buy clothes. I sat with her as we thumbed through the catalogues and she helped me choose my outfits. She then placed an order with Boans in Perth and Winns in Sydney. We were always smartly dressed kids on a trip to town, scrubbed up with hair shining. She insisted on that. Our school uniforms she ordered from Bennetts clothing store in Geraldton, from where students collected them on their return from holidays.

Packing for the term away was an exciting yet busy time. Fortunately, Mum was an organised woman, making sure we were properly equipped for the twelve weeks away. As she set about getting our individual needs sorted, Aunty Maggie and Topsy came over from Liveringa to help. I always called Aunty Maggie 'Lidgeun' and Topsy 'Nundula'. They watered the gardens, helped with the cooking and were invaluable to Mum on many levels. She would have been hard pressed to get it all done without their support. Ensuring that everything her children needed for the three months away was important to Mum. She put pressure on Dad to find the money for necessities so we were as well prepared as any other boarder.

Dad moved the blue table out to the bough shed and an old grey blanket was spread over it then covered with a bed sheet. The tabletop was now the ironing table. The three women worked tirelessly as school blouses, shirts, trousers, casuals, handkerchiefs and serviettes were washed, starched and hung out to dry. Our tunics, blazers, ties and berets they dry-cleaned while six stove irons sat heating on the Metters. Picking up a heavy, hot iron with a clasp-on handle, they wiped the base with a cloth or rubbed it in the sand to remove black heat marks. To and from the stove they sauntered in stifling heat. Our neatly packed cases included enough toiletries for the term while small hampers of biscuits, vegemite and condensed milk found their way into the suitcases. During the term, a food parcel would arrive with the usual trimmings and Mum's delicious chilli, onion and apple relish. Mango season fell in the last school term and Dad always sent a box down. I shared mine with my friends and Pepita sold hers to her friends.

As the plane descended over farmlands into Geraldton, the spectacle of coloured mosaic paddocks that disappeared into the horizon was in stark contrast to the tidal marshlands near Derby, where the mighty Mardoowarra and its tributaries, like giant earthworms, slithered into the King Sound. It was already late afternoon and a cool breeze greeted us as we stepped from the plane. I shivered and moved closer to my sister.

From the airport we went straight to Marine Terrace to collect my uniforms from Bennetts. Standing in the main street, I stared at the huge two-storey buildings that seemed to engulf us. Like my Aunty Gertie many years before on arrival in Perth, my little head turned every which way. 'Jacinta, do you want an ice-cream wedge?' Pepita's voice broke my gawking. It sounded and looked nice. A thick slice of strawberry ice-cream wedged between two wafers. But I wasn't feeling well after the long flight. No-one realised how much I would be affected by air sickness. Sure, I suffered from car sickness, so Mum always carried a bottle of Dexal, an anti-vomiting powder that you mixed with water to make a fizzy drink. It settled me on long road journeys. But now I had no such relief.

The college stood a block or two back from Marine Terrace, Geraldton's main street. I was in awe of a building that loomed like a fortress high on a hill as we drove towards it in the taxi. From the second floor, looking back beyond Marine Terrace, you could see the Indian Ocean, hence the name of the college, 'Stella Maris – Star of the Sea'. The college is still there today but not as an all-girls' school. It became co-ed in February 1994 and the name changed to Nagle College, after the founder of the Presentation Sisters in Ireland, Nano Nagle. Neither Stella Maris nor St Pats exist as residential colleges anymore.

Two Irish nuns greeted us: Sister Delores, who looked after the 'big ones', including Pepita and my cousins; and Sister Veronica, who was in charge of us 'little ones' in the Sacred Heart dormitory on the first floor. How that woman ever coped is almost unfathomable. When I had two small children of my own, I came to appreciate what the twenty-year-old nun had been shouldered with. Not only was she inadvertently a surrogate mother to twelve young children, she was the Year 1 teacher. The college had mostly day scholars and there were up to 100 children in her class. It's no wonder she lost the plot with us and didn't hesitate to crack the cane across our arms and legs.

That first year away was a dramatic departure from my early childhood trajectory – evident by my school reports that Dad had kept. I failed in most areas, but by the second year I had improved considerably. My parents were advised, almost straight away, that I should learn the art of speech. Pepita was already doing the extracurricular subject. My Aboriginal English and Kriol were treated like any foreign language that needed to be corrected. I hated Speech and Drama classes – but I had no choice. Home on school holidays one year I begged my parents to let me drop it and they said yes, but neglected to tell the nuns. 'Well, your parents haven't told us!' So it was on with learning to mime and rehearse poems and prose by heart to recite in front of an examiner from Perth. In fact, our parents agreed with anything the nuns and brothers recommended. They placed unconditional trust in their decisions. I spent more time under the care of Catholic nuns than I did my own parents given that for nine months each year, over the nine scholastic years, I was at boarding school. Mum wrote to us regularly, sending pocket money that the nuns put into a kitty so we didn't spend it all at once.

Day scholars' parents volunteered to cover my books and writing pads. Neatly covered with brown paper and a holy picture stuck onto it, my name was beautifully scribed across the top then covered with plastic. Each morning as we sat down at our desks, I printed at the top of my pad A.M.D.G. (All My Duties are done for God). The following year I began violin lessons. Pepita was already learning to play the piano and Shirley played the banjo. My parents bought a three-quarter-sized fiddle for me. Unlike most of the nuns, who came from Ireland, our music teacher was from Geraldton. Sister Vianney 'Gwen' Sivwright – the nun I stayed closest to during my years at the college.

Kimberley kids didn't go home for short breaks. It was just too far and costly. I sometimes went with boarders on long weekends and at Easter to their farms, while it was the day scholars who took me to their homes on the first Sunday of each month. I missed Easters at Debesa, where I was up at daybreak to see the sun dance across the sky and spawn pulsating tinges of colour through thin clouds. That, my parents promised, was a sure sign Jesus had arisen from the dead. And if I got up even earlier, I might glimpse Him rising into Heaven escorted by angels. But I never did. Only half believing them, I was content enough to crack open and suck on sweet, hard, icing-glazed Easter eggs the size of emu eggs.

Sometimes I wondered whether my parents had been overprotective during our formative years, given our sheltered upbringing between a small, isolated sheep station, with few people, and same-sex boarding schools. Our social interactions were limited to the three school terms in Geraldton, totally constrained by dormitory living, the college boundary fence and homesickness. Realistically, however, it was the best option if we were to receive a half-decent education while they met the challenges of running their station.

———

Shortly before Mr Miller arrived at Debesa for a regular visit in early June 1961, this time with Mary Durack and their youngest son, Johnny (Johnson), Leo Gugeri the driller completed a second bore that Dad was pleased to find had good-quality water too. He named the windmill Millers. The other he called Leos in honour of the reliable and well-liked driller.

It was the first time Mrs Miller, as we called her, had been to the station and her visit delighted Dad. Little did he know she considered her husband's involvement at Debesa as nothing more than a hobby. She did not seem to mind that he was spending money on the property – so long as the old boy was happy. But to my parents Debesa was no hobby. It was much, much more. It was their idyllic family home. It was the place that shaped their livelihood, and it was where they belonged and had planned to live for the rest of their lives.

As people from marginalised backgrounds, my folks had a very different view of Debesa to that of members of Western Australia's social elite, like the Millers. Unlike the failed Dampier Downs where the couple had tried to make a go of living off the land, my Dad had been fastidiously developing his lease since 1952, long before Mr Miller approached him in Derby in 1958 searching for a small pastoral enterprise in which to invest in retirement. Dad had always held the view, even before Miller's arrival, that an adequately functioning station would take time to build while he worked intermittently off site in the region to secure an income.

The Millers had arrived during the night. The next morning, Mr Miller got down to manual labour working on the tower of Visita's mill while Dad and a stockman mustered the dam paddock, searching for stragglers. Johnny and Phillip disappeared into the bush, exploring and chasing make-believe fiends through the scrub. In reality, they terrorised gnunudas and gerbardas with crude spears made from branches and they took aim at birds with their shanghais.

Mum stirred a lamb stew as Mrs Miller sat and chatted with her in the kitchen. The writer had been commissioned by the Bishop of the Broome Diocese, John Jobst, to record the expansion of Catholic missions and churches in the Kimberley. Mary Durack took every opportunity to talk with ex-mission inmates during her research. The book is called *The Rock and the Sand* and it became a valuable historical account of the region.

———

In early July, a change in the sheep was troubling Dad. Ewes were lambing late and some died just as they were about to give birth. He reported these events to the Agriculture Department and a vet from Camballin inspected them. Perhaps it was because it had been so dry, they decided. The chief West Australian veterinarian, after examination, confirmed their suspicions. Dad took to his diary, 'The same old story, lack of green feed for the ewes that are carrying lamb'. The wool industry in the Kimberley at this time was becoming less economically viable.

My parents continued to work the station to the best of their capabilities while our extended families maintained strong moral support. They often visited Debesa. During holiday time, the Puerts spent a few days between Debesa and Willumbah and the Spanish families came over from Camballin. Even Mr Miller enjoyed our families' company when they coincided with his visits.

As usual, for Christmas of 1961 we went to midnight mass in Derby, exchanged presents with the Puerts, and Dad and Tom enjoyed a nip of sherry before we made the long trek home in the early hours. Mum hardly slept a wink. She was up at daybreak preparing a feast. Roasts, cold ham, salads, trifle, plum pudding, custard, ice-cream, jelly and cordial. I helped my siblings hang balloons, tinsel and streamers from the spinifex ceiling in the bough shed. In the evening we went to Camballin to wish the Galician family un moi Feliz Nadal (a very Merry Christmas).

Christmas, Debesa, 1961 © Frank Rodriguez, photographer

That year, Pepita and I stayed on with Joe and Visita for a few days while Mum, Dad and the boys returned to Debesa. Visita was a clever dressmaker and she designed and made lovely frocks for us from the same navy blue and white striped material, one fashioned to suit a teenager and the other for a little girl. I thought I looked so beautiful in my dress as I twirled around in a world of my own, not caring who was watching. We enjoyed staying there as we grabbed our towels and flitted across the hot, red dirt and spinifex to the communal pool with the sloping walls, some distance from the houses. Jumping in at the shallow end it was the perfect relief from the stifling, wet season build-up. Yet this time almost ended in tragedy. My sister and I nearly drowned.

Most gudia families had gone south for the holiday and we had the pool to ourselves. Pepita decided to teach me to swim. After all, she had learned to swim in less calm waters in Geraldton, enduring the fury of stingers, wading over mounds of seaweed and swallowing excessive amounts of salt water. We got into difficulty. When I could no longer touch the bottom of the pool, I panicked. She managed to push me towards the side of the pool but I kept slipping back down the sloping walls into the deep and panicking even more. As she tried to push me out, she noticed a wide pump hose at the deep end, half in the water. Desperately, Pepita steered me across so we could pull ourselves out. But the hose wasn't attached to anything and the whole tube fell into the pool, with us on the end. I was terrified. I didn't want to die. Trying to climb onto her head, pushing her down as she desperately tried to come up for air, swallowing gallons of water, I was only concerned with saving myself. Somehow, she managed to propel us to the ladder, and we heaved ourselves out to safety.

Frightened and crying, we headed back to the house. Pepita, light-headed, staggered and kept collapsing onto the hot ground and vomiting. I was fine. As soon as we made it to the house we begged to go home, refusing to say what had happened – just that we wanted to go home. To his diary Dad speculated, 'Pepita y Jacinta were brought back from Camballin by Julio. They are suffering with sore ears y Pepita seems to be the worst off.'

New Year's Day was spent at Willumbah with Granny, Grampa, Kerry and the Ozies mob before visiting the barrage. The new structure was impressive, stretching across the width of the river. With the other kids I ran off to pick wild passionfruit. 'Don't eat too much of that, you kids, you'll get bellyache,' the adults warned. The small, orange-coloured fruit, the size of a cherry tomato, had a thin, crusty outer shell and black crunchy seeds embedded in a sweet, jelly-like clear flesh. They grew on a vine that had been introduced from South America earlier in the century. Today it is a pest. The rapidly growing creeper, its seeds distributed by birds and wind, smothers and strangles local plants along riverbanks across northern Australia.

Grampa with the Rodriguez and Ozies kids, Barrage, 1962.
Back row, from left: Helen, Pepita, Grampa, Franky and Roseline. Front row:
Cindy, Gary, Evelyn, Phillip and Danny © Frank Rodriguez, photographer

True to their beliefs, my parents had Sundays off – even if Dad did push the revered boundaries. We watched the stockmen saddle horses and prepare for a short muster, then skilfully manoeuvre some 300 sheep into the homestead paddock before we all set off on a picnic. Everyone piled into the Land Rover as Mum gave orders where to place the food and trappings so they survived the bush bashing, while Dad secured two hessian water bags to the front end of the vehicle and another in the back with us. After lunch he always managed a short siesta. Lying on his back on the canvas under a shady tree, hat over his face, Dad contemplated more possibilities for his station before dozing off into a gentle slumber.

He loved exploring the bush, often on foot, and he came to know his station like the back of his hand. Forever curious about what was beyond that hill, that tree and around that corner, he sometimes forgot that he had kids in tow. Exploring the Erskine hills just south of the Debesa boundary probably reminded him of the Galician mountains – it was the closest he would come to his childhood countryside. He checked on windmills and fences while we scrubbed out the troughs. A favourite picnic spot was the dam paddock that always had water. The area abounded with wildlife. Ducks skimmed the surrounding swamp's surface while flocks of brolga and ibis waded in to feed off water-soaked foliage.

On one occasion during the wet, following a decent overnight downpour, with pools of water about the paddocks and the smell of wet spinifex and sweet kangaroo grass filling the air, the Land Rover became hopelessly bogged. Dad, the risk taker, often tested Mum's patience. 'You could see that we'd get bogged going through there, Frank,' she growled. Tail between his legs, he left all of us and walked the 12 kilometres home to get the other Land Rover. Normally, he worked his way out of a quagmire by shovelling mud away from under the wheels then cramming scrub and spinifex into the shallow pit, thrusting the vehicle into four-wheel drive then pumping the clutch and revving the accelerator until it was set free. But not on this occasion. The Land Rover had to stay put until the soil dried out.

Dad, Donald Duggan, Phillip and Jose Luis Vazquez, Erskine Range © Franky Rodriguez, photographer

The first Friday of the month meant a lot to Dad and he endeavoured to get to mass with or without his family. Generally, though, we were strung along. It was the 2nd of February 1962 when we woke early to Mum's voice, 'Come on, you kids. Get up now. Mass is at eight o'clock. We have to get moving.' At 4.30 am and with no breakfast other than water, we set off. Three hours of fasting before receiving holy communion was a rule under canon law and my folks adhered to the church's regime without question – and so did we. Dressed in casuals, we hopped into the back of the Land Rover with our pillows to continue sleeping on the canvas swags. Closer to Derby, Dad pulled over at a cattle truck weigh-in bridge near Yeeda, where we dressed in our good clothes then continued on into town, arriving in time for mass.

As I knelt on the hard wooden pew, chin resting on my hands, I dozed. Suddenly, two giant black crows flew directly at my face. I screamed and then 'bang', they crashed into my head. 'Oh my God. Frank quick! Jacinta's fainted.' My head had connected forcefully with the cement floor. I was screaming as Dad picked me up and took me outside. Later, as I enjoyed a hearty breakfast at Aggie's place, a huge 'badge of honour' the size of a thumb ball protruded from my forehead. Much, much later the Catholic Church would change the rules to one hour of fasting, and eventually to no fasting at all.

The improvised Catholic church that Dad had built in 1946 from army huts was eventually replaced by a modern structure. The new church was blessed and opened on the 9th of September 1962 by Bishop Jobst. The old one had served the parish well for sixteen years, hosting weddings, baptisms, special feast days and funerals. It became a community hall for parish social gatherings and, for some years, a youth club, the 'Joybeats', where I hung out in my teens after finishing at boarding school.

———

If it wasn't for Dad's diaries, I would never have known what my folks were up to while I was away all those years at boarding school. Life in the Kimberley continued on without us. There was more happening than laborious station work. Mum continued to miss the company of her sisters and her extended family, while Dad did not know how to relax away from his work, other than on Sundays.

Phillip started school in 1963 at the Holy Rosary. He, too, stayed with the Puerts. My parents often brought him out to the station on weekends, but with him at Aggie's it gave Mum the perfect excuse to stay in town from time to time, close to her family. Dad took an occasional break as he began cementing the floor of a rotunda in the Puertollanos' backyard. Set among flourishing gardens with mango trees, a myriad of flowering plants and couch and buffalo grass, he called the building an 'outbuilding'. Everyone liked the wall-less structure with its high, corrugated-iron roof. It's where many family gatherings were held over the years.

Kimberley social gatherings included the yearly race round, an important event on anyone's calendar. People gravitated to Derby from outlying stations and towns as Dad took the workers, their families and Mum to town, returning to Debesa alone. Mum was cheerful after a stint in Derby when Dad came to pick her up after having seen us kids off to college in February 1963. She told him that she and Phillip, with Aggie, were going to Broome to see the Queen. In March the royal couple were coming to visit the Kimberley on their Australian tour. The two women got caught up in the excitement and made plans that included Tom. He would drive them to Broome. He had no choice in the matter.

Mr Miller had already written to Gare about the impending royal tour, complaining about the cash flow into the town for the Queen's ninety-minute visit. Even the front of the jail, he winced, was being made to look like a happy home with the cells hidden behind a tin fence. He claimed that an influx of people would likely top the local population. As the royal ship *Britannica* berthed at the old Broome jetty, and the royal couple flew in from having visited the north and east Kimberley communities of Kununurra and Cockatoo and Koolan islands, Derby people travelled by road to Broome. With recent rains and the unusual amount of traffic, the gravel main road between the two towns turned into a quagmire and several vehicles became bogged. The royal visit was of no interest to Dad, 'All day shearing. Katie did see the Queen in Broome, after having some trouble to get there due to bad roads.' By the time we received Mum's letter about the visit, the royal party had already been to Geraldton. There, we had lined up in school uniform on

The 'outbuilding', Puertollanos' home, Derby, 1960
© Julio Vazquez, photographer

the Geraldton Senior High School oval as they drove around in an open short-wheelbase Land Rover, waving at the crowd as their ship, moored in the Geraldton harbour, gazed down over small fishing boats.

I was returning to Stella Maris for my third year away in 1963. Back to being away from my beloved parents and suffering with homesickness. I protested about going back but it fell on deaf ears. Dressed in college uniform, an oversized blazer that boasted the school's crest and a beret pulled over my head, we awaited the announcement to board MMA's DC-3 for Geraldton. I tried again, begging to stay, but all the crying in the world didn't change my parents' minds. I walked slowly to the plane, climbed the stairs without looking back, tears rolling down my face. I leaned forwards and trudged up the stilted aisle to the third row. The tears stopped as I buckled up. It was the point of no return. Once again, like my mother before me on the boat journey to Drysdale River, I would have to endure torturous travel sickness. An eight-hour 'milk run' south before I was delivered into the care of the Presentation Sisters.

The first stop was Broome. Then Port Hedland, Roebourne and onto Wittenoom Gorge. As the plane descended over Wittenoom, thermals from the Hamersley Range caused the plane to bounce around like a helium-filled balloon. I thought I would die from air sickness. Unable to keep anything down, I vomited nothing but bile. On the ground a hostess guided me down to sit on the bottom rung of the steps to take in the 'fresh' air – of the asbestos mining town. The flight continued on to Onslow, Minnie Creek Station and Carnarvon then, after what seemed like an eternity, to Geraldton.

During the holidays one year, we spent a few days in Broome so Dad could dismantle a tank that Mr Miller had bought for Debesa. Things were continuing to wane in the wool industry as Dad mulled over a telegram before we left for Broome. The price of wool was not good. In fact, it was very low. We camped in the Miller's spare house and hung out with Marie Rose and Johnny while Dad set to work on the tank, with Franky helping him. Later, Mr Miller took us to the airport to see his small beloved Wackett – the single-engine plane with the call sign VH-AIY, the very one that he had flown over Debesa to deliver the tyre. Shielding their eyes and smiling, Broome folk looked to the sky whenever they heard the plane drone overhead with the old aviator at the controls. Mum stayed behind with Mrs Miller, revealing more about life at Beagle Bay and about Nygumi. In her journal, Mrs Miller described Mum as being 'the salt of the earth' whose children were clean and impeccably dressed.

At one point, the four of us were all boarding away in Geraldton at the same time. On the 19th of February 1965 Phillip found himself with his three siblings on the plane to Geraldton. He settled in well enough, visiting me every Sunday just in time for Sr Veronica to give him some of my pocket money.

Academically, Pepita was doing well and both of my brothers excelled in sport. They were cross-country champs and Franky was a good footy player, while Phillip's basketball prowess was clearly evident later in Derby. 'Blue baby syndrome' had little effect on my youngest sibling. He not only grew into a strong and healthy young man, but he was also musically adept and played rhythm guitar, by ear, with the popular Derby band the Benning Brothers during the 1970s.

Pepita, Phillip, Cindy and Franky, Geraldton, 1966. Source unknown

When it came time to return to Geraldton, we all went to town the day before our flight – stockmen, their wives and children – to go to the pictures. The racial divide in the town was clearly marked not only by the allocation of houses, but also by demarcations in some public areas, like at the pictures and in the pubs. Two aisles divided three sections of seating at the open-air cinema. We always sat on the right-hand side on canvas deck chairs with mostly other 'coloured' folk, while the blackfullas wandered over to the wooden benches on the far left, and the middle section was mostly taken up by the town's elite. The cinema had a gravel floor and corrugated-iron walls along the sides. At the back (or was it the front?) was the ticket booth and the entrance. There was no wall behind the large screen, beyond which were the toilets and a barricade to prevent anyone from sneaking in for free. There was no rule about the seating, as far as I was aware, but cultural divisions at the time would dictate that white people should have the best seating, black people the worst and everyone else would sit where they could. Young people of all creeds sat together in the front few rows of the middle and right-hand sections.

When my parents headed back to Debesa the next day, Grampa travelled in convoy with them before continuing on to Willumbah. He was struggling now, unable to carry out stock work since the accident, so he contemplated an offer from the Native Welfare to take up a cooking job for residents on the Derby reserve. Given his condition, it didn't take him long to accept the position and he and Granny moved to Derby.

Debesa, being close to town, remained vulnerable to thieves. It was conveniently placed for pilferers helping themselves to our mutton. On Dad's return the stockmen told him that a man was driving along the road with a rifle. Fed up, Dad grabbed his rifle, but Mum convinced him not to approach the man. Instead, with the stockmen he saddled up and mustered sheep away from the main road fence line.

———

Mum's Nigena heritage was never in question by the stockmen who didn't hesitate to teach her young sons essential life skills. Aboriginal peoples know their connections to one another and they knew exactly who Granny and Grampa's families were. They took pleasure in teaching Dad's Aboriginal sons things they should know that their gudia father could never teach them. Franky not only learned to saddle and ride horses and muster sheep, but he also learned orientating skills blackfulla way. He learned customary survival skills and to use his instincts.

William Williams, Debesa, 1960s © Frank Rodriguez, photographer

Franky learned how to survive on bush tucker – what was edible and what was not and how to prepare food. He learned to trap a barni underground without chasing it across country. We all had a go at catching ducks in the dam paddock. Dad scattered them by firing his shotgun into the air so they flew in our direction. Belly-landing on the swamp, they skimmed the surface to the water plants. As they fed we quietly swam towards them, hiding under reeds and trying to grab their legs. I never had any luck and I'm not sure that my siblings did either. But it was fun trying.

As he grew older, Franky relished mustering with our countri-min before he headed back to college. His cultural teacher was old Jerry. As they walked together in the dam paddock with its natural camping grounds and swamps, the old man called boab trees 'planting trees'. He used to walk through this area, he told my brother, with his travelling companions. Using colloquial place names, he described how they walked from the Liveringa Ranges (Grant Ranges) through the dam area to the Meda Station Ranges (Wunaamin Miliwundi) then north to Windjana Gorge in Bunuba people's country. They carried survival tools from one location to the next, through pindan country where there were no rivers. Tools and utensils they buried at the base of the 'planting trees' for use on their return journey, and to lighten their load. Here in sandy terrain, where there are no rocks, the old man and his pupil uncovered portable tools – water containers and spearheads amid chips of stone buried below the earth. This was different to tools found in 1828 on the east of Australia, which were placed under a sheet of bark to protect them from the heat. Together, the pair dug almost a metre deep to retrieve items that were once used to grind boab nuts. 'I could guarantee that I could go to one of those boab trees now and do exactly what Jerry showed me, and say, "Well. This is one of the old planting areas", and I bet I could find tools,' Franky told me when I interviewed him in 2003.

I wondered if this was the Wunan route as described by the Worrorra, Ngarinyin and Wunambal people who live in the country to the north of Debesa. Wunan is the law passed on by the Wandjina spirits that determines the systems of sharing and trading. Franky was shown burial sites that suggested people spent many months living on the route. The dam paddock was a familiar place to my brother and now, for the first time, he was hearing stories about his Aboriginal people's relationship with a landscape that to him was meaningful from a very different cultural perspective. To Franky, the land was where sheep grazed and matured for economic purposes. He took some items home only to have them taken by a visitor to Debesa who had shown an interest in them. While it is likely that Mum and the stock workers were aware of the traditional benefits of the swamp areas, little did we appreciate its Nigena significance. It was meaningful to us for very different reasons. We were parochially attached to the dam paddock. It was where Dad hunted ducks, built dams and it was where we would swim.

Franky and Dad, Debesa, 1967 © Katie Rodriguez, photographer

Visita approached the birth of her first child in early October. Her pregnancy seemed to be progressing well, but it may not have been the case. On 29 October my parents received a letter in the roadside mailbox with the news that the baby had died. Joe called in to Debesa to confide in his uncle and my parents were extremely empathetic. The sad turn of events was reminiscent of the loss of their own first child in the Derby hospital. Joe was devastated, openly showing his grief even more than Visita. Belying this strong-willed woman's reaction, she was hurting badly. Towards the end of September the following year, the extended Fraser clan prayed fervently together in the church for Visita as she and Joe left for Perth to have her second baby. The Derby doctors were taking no chances. To everyone's delight, their son, Carlos, arrived safely on 14 October. They had three more children, two born in the Kimberley – Marise in Derby and Paul in Wyndham – while their youngest, Xavier, was born in Galicia after they returned to Spain to live.

More of Dad's nephews, from the same family, came from Spain in the 1960s – Elogio, the eldest of eight siblings, and Jesus, the second youngest. Maria, Elogio's wife, with their two young sons, Jose Luis and Fernando, joined him at Camballin. She fell in love with the place and she never wanted to leave, as she told me when I last saw her in Sydney in 1994. The family had moved to Perth then to Sydney and never returned to Galicia to live. To everyone, Jesus was simply Susu. His nickname had come about because as a toddler he couldn't pronounce his name. Today, we still call him Susu. He joined Joe and Julio in Kununurra on the Ord River development, but eventually the three brothers returned to Galicia. On their departure, Joe and his family travelled via Derby to visit their extended Australian family, the Fraser clan. Over the years, all my family have been to Galicia and some of the Spanish family have visited the Kimberley. One of Dad's grand-nephews, Jorge Rodriguez, even came to trace his tio's footsteps from New Norcia to the Kimberley.

Julio, too, had brought his wife, Milagros, to Western Australia, to Fremantle, where they ran a fish and chip shop on South Terrace. Their daughter Jackie was born in King Edward Memorial Hospital – the family, however, returned to Galicia when she was three. All have returned to visit. My Spanish families took with them in their veins, pindan dust and Mardoowarra water. They have never lost their fondness for the Kimberley.

———

In mid-1966 Mum took ill again and she was admitted to hospital, where she stayed for a couple of weeks. My older siblings were growing up and Dad allowed them to take the Land Rover to visit her. She was in hospital more and more now as she struggled with diabetes and high blood pressure. Dad realised that times were difficult at Debesa as sheep became an impossible stock option in the Kimberley. The latest bales of wool were infested with lice, then more bad luck when the last wool prices plummeted again. As the station struggled to stay above water, Mr Miller and Dad's relationship deteriorated.

Their association hit an all-time low and any shared optimism for Debesa had disappeared. Finances were stretched and Mr Miller, despite still being a strong advocate of the small landowner, began directing blame at my parents. His attitude towards the family became contemptuous. He argued, for example, that our schooling in Geraldton was unnecessary and could not be sustained given the station's deficient financial status.

His complaints about our family's lifestyle were irrational given his earlier praise of Mum's cooking and that Debesa was self-sustaining. He complained to Gare, 'They do not stint themselves in food at Debesa and to see the children carving off slabs of butter to eat bread with rich soup and roast dinner is just not trying to economise.' Ironic given the food wasn't extravagant. The bread was home baked, the roasts locally sourced and the vegetables home grown. Furthermore, he was uncomfortable with the way in which we were closely connected to our extended families, both the Nigena and the Galician. He wrote again to Gare, 'I am pretty sure that Debesa could pay its way if weekend trips to Derby and Camballin, plus schooling and less lavish food were cut.' In 1966 my three siblings did leave the boarding schools. Pepita completed Year 11 and Frank completed Year 9 while Phillip commenced at the junior high school in Derby. I was the only one to return to Geraldton in 1967.

Nigena and Galician families at Debesa, mid-1960s
© *Frank Rodriguez, photographer*

Mr Miller felt that Debesa had served my parents' purpose and that they would be better off without it. He claimed that Dad, as a qualified builder, was employable, while Mrs Rod (as he always called Mum), being an excellent cook, could get a job with the Public Works Department. The girl (Pepita) as a nurse and Franky as a bulldozer driver could get well-paid employment. Debesa, he declared, should be sold.

He then had Gare write up 'for sale' letters and contact several prospective buyers, even in the United States. Mr Miller wondered where Dad was spending money that the station did not have. It is clear from his previous correspondence that Dad never hid anything from Miller Investments. His strong Christian morals prevented that. After a couple of months he wrote to Mr Miller, frustrated and disappointed that they had been forced into an unhappy position over Debesa. He pointed out that his family were upset at not knowing what was going on. Cyril Gare informed Dad that he no longer had a legal right to anything on the station.

Dad had no time for the two bookkeepers who were not keeping him in the loop about the sale of Debesa. 'My confidence in them is nil. I don't think they are the right men to help a man in the land for up these parts,' he declared. Dad was worried about repair work to windmills and fences that he could see were being hampered by the way in which Miller Investments personnel ran business. There were tanks to be cemented, new pipes and pumps to be replaced on at least four windmills and fences to be replaced that had been destroyed in bushfires.

My father's despondency was evident by the lack of attention to his diary during 1967. He made only forty entries that year, suggesting his preoccupation with the mounting conjecture in relation to the survival of Debesa. It is also probably the reason that Grampa's passing in 1967 is not cited, despite Dad's close relationship with him. Grampa died on the 4th of July that year. He was remembered nonetheless by the Catholic Church when the parish priest, Father Vincent Finnegan, wrote to the Abbot of New Norcia. He referred to Grampa as a 'pillar of the Church' for the excellent work in the way he had engaged in preparing bush people for baptism – even right up until his death. Grampa is buried in the Derby Pioneer Cemetery near my parents' first born, Dolores. Granny, who died in the Numbala Nunga nursing home on the 7th of August 1983, is buried in the 'new' Derby Cemetery's Catholic sector.

Mr Miller responded on the 27the of March 1969, outlining difficulties in continuing with Debesa. He had retreated from his long-held positive view about small landowners, 'The small man cannot succeed in the Kimberley. Unfortunately for me, I did not fully realise the truth about that.' Miller went on to lament the takeover of MacRobertson Miller Airlines by a bigger company. Rising costs, salaries, accommodation and the sacking of thirty pilots and over two hundred engineers were all instances he highlighted in the letter that had consequences for the small businessman.

Mum, meanwhile, had made it quite clear to Mr Miller that she did not want to leave Debesa. None of us did. To my parents Debesa was their rural idyll that offered peace, tranquillity, open spaces and a sense of belonging. Neither did she want to live in a town. Miller wrote to Gare claiming, 'She seems very happy at Debesa with two old age pension natives and a man. She has no work to do at all and plenty of company.' Once again, Miller had demonstrated his indifference to our extended Aboriginal families. Following a visit to Debesa in May, he again wrote to Gare about the state of affairs as he saw it. Frank, he said, was complaining that he could not pay the Aboriginal stock workers. Roustabouting was an easy job by Mr Miller's reckoning, picking the wool up and throwing it onto the sorting table. A couple of stock boys were doing the mustering and an old-aged native woman (Aunty Maggie) doing the cooking because Mrs Rod, with her usual diabetes trouble, was in Derby. Perhaps the situation in 1969 exacerbated my mother's health as she was hospitalised for two months. She did return to Debesa not expecting to leave, but within a short time my parents were living in Derby.

Following their departure, Mr Miller needed the Aboriginal workers, though he had never really connected with us as Aboriginal people and my parents were never totally comfortable in his company. Franky at just seventeen remained at Debesa and Miller relied heavily on him, even though he had placed his inexperienced son Andy, who was married with a baby son, as the manager. With no station management experience himself, Miller had little faith in his son despite Andy doing his best to please his father. Miller was missing my Dad's expertise while being grateful Franky was there to help.

After my folks left Debesa, the station was clearly collapsing under the new management and Mr Miller missed the aptness of the Rodriguez men. He believed the way to succeed was for Andy to maintain amicable working relationships with Franky, while he was suspicious of Dad. Nonetheless, he hoped that Dad would help with windmill repairs. Mr Miller had become bitter towards my father and felt that he owed him.

Dad, on the other hand, felt that Miller and Gare had misled him. In March Mr Miller wrote with presumptuous tone to Gare, 'Liveringa are quoting their sheep at $1.50 with wool on, at $1.00 off sheared. That $3,000 dollars we are paying Frank would have brought 3,000 sheep. Frank, by the way has contracts at Liveringa, rebuilding and building new quarters etc, getting well paid and I bet putting off any chance of a sale of Debesa to them.'

Dad began working at nearby Ellendale Station and he only returned to Debesa to support Franky on various jobs and to relocate our possessions to town. His diary reveals, 'In the morning went to Derby with the truck from Debesa taking most of the gear. And today we shifted into the new duplex state house. T.G.' They had been forced from their home. Forced from their 'place'.

Before long my parents realised that they could have stayed at Debesa despite the financial situation, given that the property fell into disarray soon after their departure. Within two years Miller Investments sold Debesa to sheep station owners from near Shay Gap in the Pilbara. By 1973 the new owners had abandoned the property and the lease was returned to the state government, still in the Miller and Rodriguez names. Through bureaucratic bungling Debesa remained on the Miller Investments books until the late 1970s. During this time the homestead became a camp for interlopers.

CHAPTER 8

Beyond Debesa

My folks missed their independence and they missed the
privacy of their own place away from the bustle of town life

For the second time in their lives, my parents' home was a state house. Their brand-new three-bedroom duplex wasn't in the middle of bush abounding with stock and wildlife. It was on an eighth of an acre block, a far cry from the 56,000 acres that was Debesa. The Rowan Street house, nestled on the western edge of the Derby peninsula on which the town had emerged, overlooked a tranquil, seemingly desolate marsh.

My folks missed their independence and they missed the privacy of their own place away from the bustle of town life. They missed station life. They missed their home. We all did. No longer was there the demanding routine of physical hard work, nor the satisfaction of working with sheep that had been their existence for fifteen years. The two immediately set about establishing the gardens. They planted lawns, trees, shrubs, a vegetable garden and a hedge around the front yard for privacy from the street.

Slightly elevated, the peninsula is surrounded by sprawling mudflats peppered with driftwood, mangroves and tidal creeks that offer alluring fishing spots. At the end of the peninsula the arch-shaped jetty protrudes into the King Sound, embracing one of the highest tide variations in the world. Long gone was the small jetty from where my grandparents had been taken early in the century on the steamship *Koombana*.

Approximately 250 kilometres west of Derby, tides rush from the Indian Ocean into the expansive King Sound, which channels huge volumes of water to heights of 11 metres during high tide and 2 metres at low tide. The water laps at the buttresses of the new Derby jetty, another popular fishing spot. But it was the tidal creeks that lured my Dad. When the tide was out, he drove his Holden ute over the crusty mudflats to throw his net across a creek, hauling in anything from barramundi, salmon, catfish and mullet to mud crabs.

The marsh appealed to people for different reasons. In the evenings my sister and I walked across the open landscape – our cats following, ducking in and out of clumps of grass – to sit on driftwood and gaze back towards the town. We took in the splashes of green foliage that partially hid the houses and offset the marsh. Others used their creative talents to carve driftwood into amazing objects, like coffee-table stands and sculptures that decorated front yards.

In country towns, locals are good at improvising and making the most of the natural and human-made assets. Derby folk were no exception. For young adults, the marsh and gravel pits on the outskirts of town were the perfect venues for nightlife, parties and socialising, while the Boab Festival committee in 1978 came up with the idea of organising a mud football match. They engaged the shire council to grade a football-sized oval in the marsh on the northeastern side of the town, off Villiers Street, and the Volunteer Fire Brigade filled it half a metre high with water. The event is now played on the other side of the peninsula, off Rowan Street where my folks had lived, and is an annual fixture on the town's social calendar.

Derby people have a lot of pride in the peninsula's unique-ness. Its landscape of red earth is complemented with woody eucalyptus, shrubs and myriads of boab trees. A variety of distin-guishing landmarks and events have been named in honour of the boab tree. The Boab Festival began in 1961 and it remains a significant event, while in 1970 a new hotel was named the Boab Inn. The *Derby Boab News*, first published in 1977, has changed names a few times over the years.

At fifty years of age neither of my parents were old enough for the aged pension. They would have to find jobs. Finding work had never been a problem for Dad so they weren't about to panic. Moreover, they had always been frugal. Their childhoods – Mum on a mission and Dad in a peasants' village – meant that they never craved materialistic riches, like flash cars or fashionable clothes, extravagant holidays or friends in the know. Neither came from an affluent background so there was no inheritance to look forward to. Moreover, our schooling expenses did not leave anything for any long-term retirement plans.

Our wonderful parents had instilled in us a strong work ethic that prepared us to be independent individuals. By 1970 Pepita was a registered nurse and was working at Bungarun, Franky had joined MMA as a persa-loader and I was a phonogram operator at the post office. Phillip continued his education at the Derby junior high school and during the holidays he helped Dad on building sites.

Countrimin off pastoral stations migrated to Derby during the mid-1900s after being displaced by government interventions. My extended Fraser family may not have embraced Indigenous kinship patterns per se but we supported our 'full-descent' families. Even though Aunty Maggie, Topsy, Patsy and Dickie lived on the opposite side of town, on the Derby Reserve, it didn't stop them from coming to visit Mum and Dad. Aunty Maggie sometimes slept over when Dad worked away. 'I come stay wid Mummy,' she told me. 'She sick one.' Aunty Maggie probably knew more than anyone else, other than Dad, how sick my mother was.

Lidgeun – Aunty Maggie with Pat, Cindy, Frank & Cassie, Numbala Nunga, Derby, 2003 © Pepita Pregelj, photographer

Aggie was a wonderful advocate for our families on the reserve, always making sure they had enough food, clothes and basics.

Much earlier, in the 1950s, she and Tom had taken out permits to employ individuals off the reserve. Since they both had citizenship rights, they were eligible to employ Aboriginals using a permit that was issued from either the Department of Native Affairs or the police station. They did this on a few occasions. On the 4th of April 1951, Aggie applied to have twelve-year-old Ada work for her. 'Visited by Mrs. Puertollano re permit for Ida [sic] who was lolling around Transient camp when C.N.A. in Derby, she is apparently quite capable of working and is doing a good job for Mrs. Puertollano', the clerk wrote in the department's journal. Ada was in fact a relative, therefore Aggie had an ulterior motive to employ her. She wanted Ada with her so she could care for her. Ada had been admitted to the native hospital in Derby and then discharged to fend for herself in the transient camp. She had lost the ability to speak and was suffering post-traumatic stress from an incident that wasn't disclosed by the department. Ada lived with the Puertollanos until her death. She remained loyal to Aggie and was loved and respected by our extended Fraser family. A lot of people lived in the Puerts' backyard until they could move to the reserve. They helped around the place and worked with Tom and Cyril on various civil contract work in Derby. Aggie and Tom provided a bough shed with beds and cooking facilities for them.

Patsy and Dickie had moved to Derby after Kim and Pat Rose left Liveringa in 1961 and they lived in Granny and Grampa's yard in Hensman Street until a tent became available for them on the reserve. That tent was their home for two years. The Yambos did menial jobs for the Catholic church, across the road from my grandparents' place, and their kids went to the Holy

Rosary School. Not a lot changed after they moved into town. They were still paid with flour, sugar and tea. The Department of Native Welfare and the State Housing Commission, in the meantime, made feeble attempts to provide proper housing on the reserve. Still today, life is second rate for blackfullas in the town and around the country.

Philip, Dickie, Lisa, Jessica, Patsy Yambo and Aggie, Derby Reserve, September 2003 © Cindy Solonec, photographer

With their Catholic convictions unfaltering, Mum and Dad continued to be involved in the church. They lived by the mantra, 'The family that prays together, stays together.' Their faith contributed not only to the stability of our family but also to the town's close-knit Catholic congregation. Dad's diaries often reflect those times.

But it was my parents' interaction with us regardless of where we lived that was prominent for them for the rest of their lives. Our upbringing ensured our behaviour over the years was guided by Christian values and morals. When we decided to marry, there was never any question whether we would marry in a Catholic church or not. We just did. All the grandchildren were born in either Derby or Kununurra and all were baptised as Catholics.

Franky, Phillip, Cindy, Pepita, Dad and Mum, Derby, 1986
© Jackie Rodriguez, photographer

Between 1972 and 1985 the four of us presented Mum and Dad with ten grandchildren. Pepita with Michael Hugo had Peter and Frances, and with her second husband, Bert Pregelj, Joseph arrived. Frank and Jackie Wonnacot have three children – Pepita, Shelley and Kim. Dieter and I have two, Kylie and Tammy, as do Phillip and Lyn Henderson – Roweena and Andrew. Despite all being baptised, the grandchildren did not necessarily receive further sacraments. Catholic traditions gradually waned and not all the great-grandchildren are baptised today – nor do they go to church or Catholic schools, much to Dad's disappointment. But he understood the change in attitudes in his descendants as secular influences and further education challenged our worldviews.

———

Dad continued working at Liveringa before deciding to try out for a government job. In 1971 he started working for the Main Roads Department, thus beginning a new phase in his working life, albeit a brief one. He took up employment as a bulldozer driver. Working on the Great Northern Highway 400 kilometres south of Derby, close to the Eighty Mile Beach and to Anna Plains and Nita Downs stations, he enjoyed this time. He found himself back in the bush, making roads. He was in his element. The Main Roads camp near Anna Plains was 250 kilometres south of Broome and from there he would travel to the access road into Nita Downs, where he bulldozed scrub away from the road verge to clear a path for the Bell Brothers' scrapers to dig trenches. Using his masonry skills, he built grids (run-throughs) on the fence lines to prevent stock from wandering onto the main road, and he built cement crossings over floodways.

Dad maintained a strong work ethic and, as at Debesa, he was forever busy. While working in the area he dismantled a tank at nearby Talgarno for the Derby businessman Colin Campbell. Talgarno no longer exists, but it has an interesting backstory. It was a small, well-resourced ghost town that had been built to support a British rocket venture. In 1946 under the Anglo-Australian Joint Venture, the Australian government had agreed for the British government to engage in rocket-launching trials from Woomera in South Australia. Woomera is an Aboriginal word for a throwing spear with a long trajectory. The rockets were to be projected 2,000 kilometres across the outback towards the Eighty Mile Beach, plummeting somewhere on Anna Plains. The *Black Knight* and the *Blue Streak* rockets were to soar over the Gibson and Great Sandy deserts then plunge into an area that had been proclaimed the 'Talgarno Prohibited Area' in 1958. Well, that was the plan.

The exclusion zone meant that the Yulparija people were forced from their homelands. Talgarno was built to accommodate 6,000 specialist personnel and support crews. By the 1960s it was complete with a runway and cyclone-proof structures, including a school, hospital and houses. But the British rocket experiments never happened. With the onset of the Cold War, technological advances saw the USA's superior weaponry outclass the British/Australian venture and it consequently folded. Like at Noonkanbah twenty years earlier, local people benefited from Talgarno's disused infrastructure. Colin Campbell bought materials to build a roadhouse alongside the Mardoowarra near Willare Bridge, 70 kilometres south of Derby, while the Mangrove Hotel in Broome emerged from Talgarno's disused buildings.

Camping close to the Eighty Mile Beach, Dad found time to savour the peacefulness and to fish off the reefs. But generally on weekends he took the long journey home. His time with the Main Roads didn't last too long and his diary entries hint at his awkwardness in his new workplace. As a committed Catholic and someone who valued his personal space, my dad observed behaviours of others that were different to his own.

At Debesa he had mostly worked by himself. Communal living in the Main Roads camp appears to have been alienating for him, 'the cook play up and seems to be on the way out is on the metho ... dios nos perdone God forgive us.' On another occasion he suggested to a co-worker that siphoning petrol from the work vehicles was stealing. He was told in no uncertain terms to mind his own business.

My dad did not slip easily into a culture of hard-drinking labourers and when he was transferred to a road gang near Fitzroy Crossing to cement floodways, he remained at the camp when the others headed to the Crossing. He described the work culture, '[m]ost of the men went into Fitzroy tonight to spend their pay'. Two days later he continued, 'did some hours of work as most of the men not fit for work after been drinking all night'. Dad worked hard despite the temperature and, while he enjoyed a beer, he knew his limits. By the 14th of January 1972 he had resigned and on the 20th of January he recommenced at Liveringa. He leaves no hint that he was dissatisfied with his decision to leave the government job.

———

Whenever Dad met his countryman, he enjoyed having a chinwag in his lingo. Spanish speakers in the West Kimberley were few and far between so in 1972 when he met Maria Damboronia, a domestic at the Crossing Inn, he introduced her to Mum. She became a friend of the family. Maria was from San Sebastian in Basque Country, not far from Galicia, but she never returned to Spain to live. Derby became her home for the rest of her life.

On the rare occasion, Dad was asked to be an interpreter and he seized the opportunity. First, in 1974 when a Spanish-speaking businessman arrived in the Kimberley to observe cotton-growing operations at Camballin and at the Ord Irrigation Scheme, he obliged the manager of the Australian Land and Cattle Company (ALCCO) by travelling with the party. He then took Eduardo Castillo home to meet Mum. My father may not have been the most gregarious character, but my parents were hospitable folk and they relished the company of interesting people. Mum always prepared a tasty meal, while Dad was grateful for Castillo's visit.

A few months later he stood as an interpreter in a court case for a young Spaniard. He explained the case this way, 'went to the courthouse to interpret for a Spanish chap about some trouble with firearms outside the Boab Inn fighting with drunk natives, as they want some money from him. His name is Francisco Epelde from Basque Country.'

It had been on Dad's mind for some time, for some years in fact, that he would like to take Mum to Galicia when the opportunity finally presented itself. After determining that a journey was within their means, they applied for passports, arranged traveller's cheques and received the first of their travel vaccinations. Like many Aboriginal people of my mum's era, this was probably when she first realised that she didn't even have an official birth certificate. Mercifully, the Diocese of Broome came to the rescue and provided her baptismal certificate, which sufficed for her passport application.

On arrival in Madrid on the 2nd of August 1974, they were met by Joe and Julio's sister, Aurora. With her husband,

Alejandro, the four of them drove north to see the rest of the family. Anticipation overwhelmed Dad so much so that he could hardly contain his excitement at the prospect of seeing his siblings again. First, they visited Jesus in Bilbao, in Basque Country, then west to Galicia, where Amable and Dolores still lived in their villages at Freixo and Nocedas respectively.

While in the area, Dad made a point of visiting the families of the Spaniards he had met in the Kimberley. They first visited Maria Damboronia's family then the parents of Francisco Epelde, the young fulla he'd helped in the Derby courthouse. Epelde's parents must have been relieved to know that a Spaniard from northern Spain had been there for their son when he found himself in a spot of trouble with the law in a foreign country – relieved that he wasn't languishing in some Australian outback jail.

They moved closer to Monforte de Lemos at the end of August, after having spent time with family in Barcelona. Now they travelled by train through the farming countryside of northern Spain into the mountainous wine-growing area of Galicia. Mum was in awe. Fascinated by the vineyards terraced into the sides of the mountains, she half listened to Dad's incessant chatter about his home country. He even took her to meet his childhood friends in Monforte before going out to Freixo. Paca (Francesca), one of Amable's ten children – she had nine daughters and one son – with her husband, chauffeured them around the Monforte countryside,

> *Today at last got to Frejo [sic]. Paca's husband took us up there*
> *on her car. It has been a happy day to be able to see home again*
> *after so many years over 37. Paca and her children was a great*

happiness to be with them. The house was much changes, but the neighbourhood is very much the same people not so many left. Perdigon – Pepe dos de Arribo shoquin. Salgueiro y familias also paid a visit to the chapel. Was nice to see the old chapel again.

Freixo, huddled in the mountains, is susceptible to forest fires and Dad spent time helping fight fires during their short stay. He knew only too well how to fight bushfires. It was something he had done on a regular basis at Debesa, making firebreaks and burning off bush in readiness for rejuvenation during the wet. They then headed to La Coruña to meet his nephews. Finally, they visited Samos – rekindling Dad's childhood memories at the Benedictine monastery.

Jose Rodriguez, Mum, Dad, Amelia and Jesus Rodriguez, Bilbao, 1974. Photographer unknown

Satisfied at having at last returned to Spain with Mum, he booked their return journey via Rome, Hong Kong and Darwin. On the 10th of September they arrived back in Derby. A large group of people gathered at the airport to greet them on their return, eager to hear tales of a mysterious Spain.

———

Life quickly returned to normal at home. Dad engaged with contract work and occasionally he worked on the wharf. Mum controlled the household duties and she regularly interacted with her extended family. Like at Debesa, my parents enjoyed their Sunday outings. On drives out to the river they sometimes stopped to watch the waterskiers on a man-made lake near the Willare Bridge. It's where my brothers and I, behind Dieter's speed boat, learned to ski. Passers-by stopped to try their luck at skiing or to show off their fishing haul. The lake is gone now, replaced by a steel bridge. The levee banks that had created the chance ski lake were washed away by floodwaters continuing on their natural trajectory, filling the tributaries of the mighty Mardoowarra. Nonetheless, the skiers' legacy remains. The bridge is called Ski Lake in honour of us who skied there in the 1970s, its history unknown to the hundreds of travellers who pass over the bridge each year, likely wondering how in the hell this place got its name.

Ski Lake, Great Northern Highway, Mardoowarra, 1975. Source unknown

By the 1970s my parents' heritages, Nigena and Galician, had long been part of their lifestyle. Their like-minded worldviews had played a major part in strengthening who they were as a couple. While government policies evolved around them, my parents took any changes in their stride. They were aware of Australian politics and national and world news through radio and newspapers and copies of the Catholic *Record* that were scattered around their home. Dad often had the *El País* sent to him by someone in Perth and he enjoyed *Time*, the *Reader's Digest* and *National Geographic*. We never actually sat around discussing politics. Our often lively and robust conversations around the table, in the lounge and on the lawns of my parents' Rowan Street home were about local issues and family.

Dad rarely showed his emotions but when his best mate Tom Puertollano died in August 1978, Mum asked if he'd be going to the novena and he broke down. Sitting at the dining-room table with tears streaming down his face, I was at a loss as to what to say. 'Tommy's gone. Who am I going to talk to now?' Tom left a big gap in my Dad's life. He already missed Grampa and now Tom, who had always been there for my folks as they laboured to develop Debesa, was gone too. Moreover, his children had begun an exodus from Derby, so he and Mum often travelled by road to visit us. Most trips were to Kununurra, where Franky lived after he had transferred there with MMA in the late 1970s. Dad used those visits to the East Kimberley as a working holiday, taking on small building contracts.

On one journey they had a dreadful car accident just south of Kununurra. It was the 25th of May 1982 when they set off from Derby in convoy with Franky and his young family returning home after holidaying near Broome. An eight-hour journey by road, they travelled into the night. Franky, travelling ahead, had been keeping a check on them in his rear-vision mirror and he became concerned when he didn't see their headlights for a while. He turned the car around and headed back. On approach they could see lights of the overturned van on the side of the road and another vehicle had come alongside. The family sat silently as they drew closer, not knowing what to expect. Dad had hit a bullock and the vehicle rolled two or three times. An ambulance, the police and tow truck arrived and Mum and Dad were taken to the Kununurra hospital. Mum had been badly injured.

Her upper chest was slightly crushed, her right foot twisted and her right big toe severely cut. Dad's injuries were less severe – his right shoulder had been battered. The van was a write-off. Mum remained in hospital for two weeks before she was well enough to be transferred to the Derby hospital. Several days later and still experiencing pain across the top of her chest, Dad noticed that her ankle had turned a dark, purplish colour. Her damaged toe had not improved and gangrene had set in. The Derby-based surgeon chipped away at the foot, removing small shreds of gangrene, but by the 17th of July he made the decision to send her to Perth for intensive care.

Mum began to hallucinate as she was transferred to Sir Charles Gardiner Hospital by RFDS on the 31st of August. Her leg was amputated and, with Dad by her side, she remained in the Perth hospital for the next six months. She struggled to regain her health as she dealt with ongoing complications while learning to walk again with the aid of prosthesis,

This morning left Sir. Charles Gairdner Hospital. Katie spent close to six months in this hospital. TG at last can come home after much suffering in nearly 8 months. Left Perth airport about 6.30 am went via Mount Newman, Port Hedland, Broome. Katie had to be transferred on the forklift from one plane to the other. Bob Noble did the handling. Got to Derby about midday, was good to be home again TG.

In October 1984 Mum returned to Perth for an eye operation and to have her prosthesis adjusted. She had been having difficulties walking and the doctors sent her down to Perth for intense physiotherapy. Gradually, she became used to the refitted prosthesis while modifications to their Rowan Street home were now necessary to accommodate her wheelchair. Dad was contracted to install handrails in the shower and the toilet and in November 1986 an electric oven was installed in the kitchen at chest height so Mum could manage cooking more easily.

Katie and Frank, Derby, 1986
© Dieter Solonec, photographer

Dad had been working at Numbala Nunga in a maintenance role when he turned sixty-five on the 7th of February 1986, becoming eligible for the aged pension. He did not slow down in retirement. He didn't know how to, as he took on small contract work around the town. He did running repairs in people's homes, at the school, in the church and for the State Housing Commission. And he took to fishing more often.

Throughout 1986 and for the next two years whenever they could, Mum and Dad went along to the Senior Citizens Club. An average of twelve people made the most of the service, meeting at various locations since there was no dedicated space for seniors. Generally, they met at the Sportsmen's Club. They enjoyed meals together and activities like carpet bowls, indoor cricket, Game of Proverbs, poker and special presentations.

Grandkids, Derby, 1986. Back, from left: Joseph, Peppi, Shelley.
Middle: Roweena, Kim, Frances, Peter, Kylie, Tammy.
Front: Andrew, Katie, Frank © Dieter Solonec, photographer

That year my parents celebrated their fortieth wedding anniversary. Mum had decided that she might not make it to celebrate their fiftieth, so she planned a celebration at the Sportsmen's Club. The Fraser family's connectedness was on display as many of us headed to Derby for the occasion. Some of Mum's siblings were there too, along with nieces and nephews from Darwin.

———

Biddy Kelly, Mum's close friend from their convent days, was a regular visitor. Mum enjoyed the company of her lifelong friend and she looked forward to visitors in general since she was pretty much housebound now. She would have lengthy yarns with her good friend Ellen Ozies over the phone, giggling about who knows what! At some point, Dad had become a Eucharistic minister, and he assisted the priest at mass by distributing holy communion to the congregation. Afterwards, he would take communion to people who could no longer go to church on Sundays – including Mum.

As time went on, she found it more and more difficult to walk on her prosthesis and mounting stairs had become unmanageable. Dad placed two narrow timber planks over the four steps from the front verandah to the lawn so he could wheel her down. She loved to sit and enjoy the afternoon breeze and watch the birds flutter in the sprinkler. Phillip's kids who lived in Derby often visited and sometimes we holidayed while visitors occasionally popped by. The planks proved not to be a good idea. On one occasion, as Dad pushed Mum up the planks, one wheel slipped off. He could do nothing but use all his strength to just hold her ample frame in the wheelchair and pray for help. They were answered when Sister Camille Poidevon, a regular visitor, stopped by at the most convenient time and helped Dad.

After this incident he built a firmer, but no wider ramp from the back door that made the task of wheeling her into the house only slightly easier. As time went on, she struggled to attach the prosthesis to her stump and walking became intolerable so she visited the doctor on the 11th of November 1988. The doctor immediately made arrangements for Mum to return to Perth to have a new leg fitted. Dad was now her full-time carer. He flew south with her as her official escort and they spent six weeks at the Aboriginal Medical Service Autumn Centre in Bayswater. Each day they travelled by taxi to the Royal Perth Rehabilitation Hospital in Shenton Park, where she once again learned to walk.

Mum's condition continued to deteriorate over the years, and it is probably only because of modern medicines that her life extended to seventy-three years. On the occasions that she had to be in Perth for ongoing medical attention, family and friends were there for her, especially my cousin Phillipa Cook and family friends Elizabeth and Bill Posthuma. They were tireless in their support. Between them they ensured that all my parents' needs were met while in the city.

As a diabetic, Mum's immune system left her more susceptible to other complications and she suffered stomach problems and ulcers developed. By the 1st of June 1989 she was admitted to the Derby hospital and immediately transferred to Perth to have a hernia removed. Dad followed after a few days. Following this operation her health was very slow to improve. He visited her each day, taking her outdoors in the wheelchair. It was two months before she was able to be transferred back to Derby.

Phillip worked as an orderly at the hospital and he helped with Mum's care. Being hospitalised in Derby was a good thing because it meant that she had regular visitors. Her children, her siblings and her extended family would travel to Derby just to be close to her. It also meant that Dad did not have to rely on other people for their hospitality as he did in Perth. There she remained until the end of August, occasionally returning home for a few hours at a time. When my mother was eventually discharged, she was so weak that a community health nurse visited daily to treat and dress her stomach wound and Dad became involved in her treatment. He would record her blood and sugar levels, take her for check-ups, and collect her prescriptions from the chemist. He became more than her carer. He was her nurse too. Overall, Dad was her devoted husband.

Nursing duties done, he continued with his daily life. Gardening, grafting mango trees, tinkering with his car, doing odd handyman jobs, writing letters and keeping in telephone contact with us. My parents had accepted their destiny in life. Their strong beliefs had conditioned them to do that and together they lived contentedly in their Rowan Street home.

In her final years Dad's domestic help ensured Mum followed a strict diabetic diet. They listened to country music and to the radio and they watched TV. Both were West Coast Eagles fans and Mum still followed the cricket. She always remembered our birthdays, reminding Dad to buy a card and to include a ten or twenty dollar note in the grandkids' cards.

This routine continued until her death in 1994. Each day Dad wrote in his diary and, just like earlier years, he would comment on the weather. In the months before she died my mother was constantly in pain. She left us early one morning on the 7th of April 1994. 'This morning about 4.30 Katie passed away at the regional hospital. Fr. Lorenz gave her last sacraments about an hour before she died. May her soul rest in the peace of Our Father & Blessed Lady most Sacred Heart have mercy on her soul!'

Epilogue

Dad visited his brothers, Jose and Manuel, in South America in 1996. Travelling on a tour bus with Jose from Buenos Aires to visit the Iguazu Falls, one of the natural wonders of the world, he likened the countryside with lots of cattle, sheep and horses to the Kimberley 'on a good wet season'. Two years later he left Derby for greener pastures to live in Kununurra, closer to Franky. It would be the first time he had lived outside the West Kimberley since his arrival in 1944, fifty-two years earlier. 'Today finished my stay in Derby or West Kimberley. This afternoon I left for Fitzroy Crossing and Frank was at the Crossing so we met there and camped for the night. I went to H. Mass in the morning said goodbye to Srs' of Saint John of God.' He remained in the Kimberley for the rest of his life, living in Kununurra and later in Broome, where he lived with Pepita.

Dad left us on the 29th of March 2011 after a stroke and a short stint in the Broome hospital, where he managed to keep everyone wondering when he would depart. The incumbent Spanish-speaking South American priest Father Ernesto and even the Catholic Bishop of the Broome Diocese, Christopher Saunders, came several times to administer the 'last rites'. One thing's for sure, my Dad not only received all the sacraments he was entitled to in his lifetime, but he was assured of a safe passage to his beloved God and to Mary, who he was devoted to.

My Dad died midway through my PhD research, leaving unfinished business. Or was it? His passing wasn't untimely, but at the right time. Questions still crop up that I wish I had answers to, but now it was up to me to complete the story with input from my siblings – and a degree of speculation.

He was pleased that his diaries were being used. Without them, this story would not have had the chronological framework to complement my family's history, thus giving comment to a social record not necessarily documented in the region – a story of marginalised peoples during the 1900s. My parents' legacy is a treasured gift from them to their descendants, extended families and friends.

———

Today, Debesa is owned by Marcia and Froggie (Owen) Finger. After selling Mowla Bluff Station in March 1995, the couple needed somewhere to 'sit down' for a while and decide where they were going. They didn't want to leave the Kimberley. So they approached their friend who owned Debesa to see if he was interested in selling, and he was.

Although not good cattle country, Debesa was fully fenced, close to town, just off the bitumen and it had 'beautiful' water with a number of bores and good, reliable rainfalls to boot. The Fingers found that not being near a river source and having no surface water was in fact an advantage. It made it easier to trap cattle at mustering times, thus reducing costs.

Marcia Finger describes the Kimberley as God's own country and, although some months can be difficult, there is nowhere else she would rather be. It has an atmosphere of wilderness similar to Africa, where she grew up. Before coming to the Kimberley in 1976 Marcia had travelled widely but she never found a sense of place anywhere else. Indeed, my Dad was satisfied that his small station had ended up with someone like Marcia. Debesa, is the Fingers' own rural idyll.

Debesa, 2010 © Cindy Solonec, photographer

Glossary

Aboriginal

barni – goanna

barrgana – the cold season in Nyul Nyul country. Strong, dry southeasterly winds from June to August

countrimin – Aboriginal people in Kriol (Kriol is the language spoken across large areas of northern Australia)

gnunuda – spiky lizard

gudia – non-Aboriginal person in Kriol. Generally, a white European

Irremugadu – Roebourne

jarramba – freshwater prawns

jila – waterhole (in Walmajarri)

kungerberry – sweet berry

Kwini/Kulari (also Cuini, Gunin, Gwiini, Gwini, Kunan and Wunambal) – country in the Drysdale River/Kalumburu region

leinju – policeman (generic Kimberley word)

liyan – deep feelings

magabalas – bush fruit

Mardoowarra – Nigena name of the lower Fitzroy River in the Kimberley

moulijin – well-chewed tobacco that is continually rolled in eucalyptus ash

nanya – Nigena for mother's breast

Ngarluma (also Ngalooma, Gnalluma, Gnalooma and Ngaluma) – country that spans from west of Karratha to the Peewah River, and from the coastline to the Millstream Chichester National Park

ngi – yes

ngili-ngilis – bush fruit

Nigena (also Njigina, Nyigina and Njigana; the orthographical spelling is Nyikina) – the country around Derby

Nygumi – Nyul Nyul for grandfather

Nyul Nyul (also Niol-Niol, Nyolnyol, Njul-Njul, Njolnjol, Nyool and Nyool Nyool) – country in the Beagle Bay coastal area

Wadjemup – Rottnest Island

Woonyoomboo – the first man to travel along the river before he became a rufous night heron in the Nigena belief system

wudjella – non-Aboriginal person

Spanish

abuela – grandmother

adios – goodbye

agua – water

azúcar – sugar

buenos dias – good day

buenos noches – good night

Camino de Santiago – Way of St James

castaña – chestnut

debesa – small paddock

donde yo soy hay muchas castañas – where I come from there are many chestnuts

el mundo – the world

gracias – thank you

grande Navedad – wonderful Christmas

leche – milk

mantequilla – butter

mi sobrini – my nephew

muchacho – boy

pan – bread

polbo – octopus

por favor – please

Pro Ecclesia et Pontifice – The Church and the Pope

salchichas – sausages

tio – uncle

tortillas de pataca – potato omelette

un moi Feliz Nadal – a very Merry Christmas

verde Espana – green Spain

Other

killer – sheep or cattle for farm workers to eat

T.G. – Thank God

treadly – sewing machine

Bibliography

PRIMARY SOURCES

Archives

Battye Library

Bauer, FH, '*Durack Family Papers, 1886–1991*', 1986, ACC819A.

Blythe, Lindsay Gordon, *Reminiscences of L.G. Blythe: Comprising of Early Life on Kimberley Stations, Airbeef and Building of Roads*, 1977.

Durack, Kim, '*Durack Family Papers, 1886–1991*', 'Kim Durack Business Correspondence 1937–1958', ACC819A.

Durack, Mary, '*Durack Family Papers, 1886–1991*', 'Diary', 1962, ACC819A.

Fletcher, Jack, '*Australian Land and Cattle Company*', Diaries, 2014, ACC7733A – restricted until the death of Jack Fletcher.

Gare, Cyril, '*Durack Family Papers, 1886–1991*', HCM/BUS2, 1956–1971, ACC819A.

Godbehear, Harold S (Harold Stephen), 1893–1976, Archival [196-?], 4th Floor Stack, ACC 7277A.

Kelleher, P, '*Historic Buildings of the Kimberley Region in WA*', 1988, Q 994.14/KIM.

Kerr, NF, *Preliminary Report on Nyigina*, 1969.

Kimberley Pastoral Company, *Records, 1891–1963*, ACC1240A.

Miller, Andrew, 'Durack Family Papers, 1886–1991', HCM/BUS2, 1956–1971, ACC819A.

Miller, Horry, '*Durack Family Papers, 1886–1991*', HCM/BUS2, 1956–1971, ACC819A.

Official Opening: Camballin Irrigation Area, 4 December, 1961.

Private Archives Manuscript, *Canning Stock Route*, History Collection, 2019.

Rodriguez, Frank, '*Durack Family Papers, 1886–1991*', HCM/BUS2, 1956–1971, ACC819A.

Department of Aboriginal Affairs

Department of Native Affairs, Fulgentius Fraser (Wife Phillipina Fraser nee Melycan), 'Personal file', item 945/40, 1940.

Department of Native Affairs, Katherine Fraser, 'Personal file', item 879/43, 1943.

Landgate

Minister for Lands, *Pastoral Lease: The Transfer of Land Act, 1893*, 1949.

Minister for Lands, *Pastoral Lease: Kimberley Division*, 1953.

Minister for Lands, *Transfer: The Transfer of Land Act 1893–1950*, 1958.

New Norcia

Benedictine Community of New Norcia, Drysdale River Mission/Kalumburu Journal, PAX Benedictine Archives, 1923, 65014P.

Catalan, IA OSB, *Personal Letter*, PAX Benedictine Archives, 15 July 1941.

Fraser, Fulgentius, *Personal Letter*, PAX Benedictine Archives, 1919.

Rodriguez, Frances – Hno Beda, PAX Benedictine Archives, 1937–1941.

Santos Ejercicios, PAX Benedictine Archives, 1937.

Pallottine

Broome Catholic Diocese, *Mary Catherine Fraser*, Baptism Certificate, 1974 (issued), EJ Dwyer, Broome.

Nailon, Brigidia, 'Nothing is wasted in the household of God', *Derby Chronicle*, SAC Pallotine Archives Rossmoyne (draft manuscript), 1939–1967.

State Records Office of Western Australia

Department of Native Affairs, Liveringa Station, 'Employment. Living and General Conditions', item 733/47.

Department of Native Affairs, Liveringa Station, 'Native Matters', item 775/38.

Department of Native Welfare, Commissioner of Native Welfare, 'Letters', 1971, item DNW71.

Department of Native Welfare, Aboriginal Consultative Committee, 'Letter – F Gare', 1968, item 1729 WYG25.1.

District Police Office (Fitzroy), JT Campbell, 'Journal', item 430/4739, 1909.

Fremantle Shipping Registers

Lands Department, Pastoral Lease Committee – a further interview with Mr Kim Rose, Liveringa Station and Mr Bill Henwood, Calwynyardah Station, 'Transcripts of Evidence', con 4983, 1962.

Smythe, PS, Native Hostels – Derby file, 'Letter', *Lands and Surveys*, item 481/51, 1958.

'Walter Fraser', 1919/107, con 3458.

Diaries

Rodriguez Snr, Frank, *Diaries*, Battye Library, Perth, 1944–1969.

Rodriguez Snr, Frank, *Diaries*, Private Collection – Cindy Solonec, 1970–2012.

Government documents

Commonwealth of Australia, *Certificate of Naturalization*, Minister of State for Immigration, Canberra, Commonwealth Government Printer, 1948.

Commonwealth of Australia, *Quarantine Service*, Department of Health, Perth, 1937, Battye Library.

Moseley, Royal Commissioner, *Report: Investigate, Report, and Advise Upon Matters in Relation to the Condition and Treatment of Aborigines*, Government Printer, Perth, 1935.

Interviews

Author's possession

Begley, Pat, interviewed by the author, 2012, notes in author's possession, Perth.

Bullough, Audrey, interviewed by the author, 2012, notes in author's possession, Perth.

Megaw, Marie Rose, interviewed by the author, 2012, notes in author's possession, Perth.

Rodriguez, Frank Snr, interviewed by the author, 1990, notes in author's possession, Perth.

Rodriguez, Katie, interviewed by the author, 1991, notes in author's possession, Perth.

Battye Library, OH3908/12 – Rodriguez and Fraser families

AhMat, Gertie, interviewed by the author, 2003.

Bergmann, Pat, interviewed by the author, 2003.

Fraser, Edna, interviewed by the author, 2003.

Fraser, James, and Rodriguez Snr, Frank, interviewed by the author, 2003.

Fraser, Leena, interviewed by the author, 2003.

Gooch, June, and Gooch, Henry, interviewed by the author, 2003.

McCarthy, Kerry, interviewed by the author, 2003.

Ozies, Tony, interviewed by the author, 2003.

Pregelj, Pepita, interviewed by the author, 2003.

Puertollano, Aggie, interviewed by the author, 2003.

Puertollano, Cyril, interviewed by the author, 2003.

Rickerby, Shirley, interviewed by the author, 2003.

Rodriguez Snr, Frank, interviewed by the author, 2003.

Rodriguez Jnr, Frank, interviewed by the author, 2003.

Ward, Frances, interviewed by the author, 2003.

Yambo, Patsy, and Yambo, Dickie, interviewed by the author, 2003.

Legislation

Aborigines Protection Act 1886
Aborigines Act 1905 (WA)
Immigration Restriction Act 1901 (Cwlth)
Native Administration Act 1936 (WA)
Natives (Citizenship Rights) Act, 1944–1951 (WA)

Newspapers

Anna Plains Cattle, Ready Sale at Meekatharra – The Pastoralist, *The Western Mail*, 6 September 1934 [Trove].
Anna Plains Cattle, Turner Test Satisfactory, Overlanding Commenced – On the Land, *The West Australian*, 18 May 1934 [Trove].

Other unpublished sources

Agricultural Department, *Certificate of Registration of Stock Brands, Brands Act, 1904–1956*, Registrar of Brands, Perth, 1954, 1960. Private collection, Cindy Solonec.
Copy of Baptism Certificate, *Agnes Eulla (Frazer) DOB 4/1/24*, Kalumburu, via Wyndham Baptismal Register, 24 September 1988, Anscar McPhee. Private collection, Helen Bergmann.
Rose, Kevan, 'Liveringa Station, Derby (Jan 1949 to Dec 1951)', in 'This Is My Life', unpublished, 2005. Private collection.

SECONDARY SOURCES

Articles and books

Aceves, Joseph, and Douglass, Williams, *The Changing Faces of Rural Spain*, New York, Halsted Press, 1976.
Allen, B, and West, P, 'Influence of dingoes on sheep distribution in Australia', *Australian Veterinary Journal*, vol. 71, no. 7, 2013, pp. 261–267.
Anderson, Jim, 'Camballin: A West Kimberley development conundrum', [online] *Early Days: Journal of the Royal Western Australian Historical Society*, vol. 12, no. 4, 2004, pp. 385–400.

Anderson, Jim, 'Liveringa Homestead Group', in Tanya Suba and John Taylor (eds), *Register of Heritage Places*, Group 10 11/12/1998 vols, 1997.

Andrews, Munya, *The Seven Sisters of the Pleiades: Stories from Around the World*, Spinifex Press, Melbourne, 2005.

Barnard, Alan (ed.), *The Simple Fleece: Studies in the Australian Wool Industry*, Melbourne University Press, Melbourne, 1962.

Barry, Amanda, 'Ernst Eugen Kramer (1889–1958)', in Regina Ganter, *German missionaries in Australia – a web-directory of intercultural encounters*, 2016, www.griffith.edu.au/missionaries.

Bauer, FH, 'Sheep raising in Northern Australia: an historical review', *Australian Geographer*, vol. 7, no. 5, 1959, pp. 169–179.

Benedictine Community of New Norcia, 'Drysdale River Mission', in St Ildephonsus College magazine, New Norcia, 1930.

Bianchi, P, *Work Completed, Canning: A Comprehensive History of the Canning Stock Route 1906–2010*, Hesperian Press, Perth, 2013.

Biskup, Peter, *Not Slaves, Not Citizens: The Aboriginal Problem in Western Australia 1898–1954*, University of Queensland Press, Brisbane, 1973.

Bolton, GC, *The Kimberley Pastoral Industry*, UWA Press, Perth, 1954.

Bolton, GC, *Alexander Forrest: His Life and Times*, Melbourne University Press and UWA Press, Melbourne, 1958.

Bolton, GC, 'The Emanuels of Noonkanbah and GoGo', *Early Days*, vol. 8, no. 4, 1980, pp. 5–21.

Bouema, Gary D, *Mosques and Muslim Settlement in Australia*, Brown Prior Anderson, Canberra, 1994.

Boyd, Annie, *Koombana Days*, Fremantle Press, Fremantle, 2013.

Bridge, P, and Dreezens, G (eds), *The Drover's Scrapbook*, Hesperian Press, Perth, 2008.

Broad, Nan, 'The Eighty Mile Beach: false promise and harsh reality', *Early Days: Journal of the Royal Western Australian Historical Society*, vol. 12, no. 6, 2006, pp. 602–615.

Brodie, Nick, *Under Fire: How Australia's Violent History Led To Gun Control*, Hardie Grant Books, 2020.

Broken Hill Proprietary Company, 'The decade 1945–1955', *Seventy-five*

Years of B.H.P. Development in Industry, 1885–1960 / BHP (firm) Broken Hill Proprietary, Melbourne, 1960.

Buxton, Nicholas, *Tantalus and the Pelican: Exploring Monastic Spirituality Today*, Continuum International Publishing Group, London/New York, 2009.

Capell, A, 'Australia social anthropology: notes of the Njigina and Warwa tribes, N. W. Australia', *Mankind*, vol. 4, no. 11, 1953, pp. 450–469.

Chalarimeri, Ambrose, and Tan, Traudl, *The Man from the Sunrise Side*, Magabala Books, Broome, 2001.

Choo, Christine, 'The role of the Catholic missionaries at Beagle Bay in the removal of Aboriginal children from their families in the Kimberley region from the 1890s', *Aboriginal History*, vol. 21, 1997, pp. 14–29.

Choo, Christine, *Mission Girls: Aboriginal Women on Catholic Missions in the Kimberley, Western Australia, 1900–1950*, UWA Press, Perth, 2001.

Clarke, Philip, *Where the Ancestors Walked: Australia as an Aboriginal Landscape*, Allen & Unwin, Sydney, 2003.

Conor, Liz, 'Black velvet and purple indignation: print responses to Japanese poaching of Aboriginal women', *Aboriginal History*, vol. 37, 2013, pp. 51–77.

Cornish, Hamlet, *Pioneering in the Kimberley*, Hesperian Press, Perth, 2011 (pp. 5–7).

Cresswell, Tim, *Place: A Short Introduction*, Blackwell Publishing, Oxford, 2004.

Daly, Alphonsus M, *Healing Hands: Memories and Milestones of the Derby Leprosarium, where Sisters of St. John of God Provided Nursing Care*, Health Department of Western Australia, Perth, c. 1986.

Davidson, WS, *Havens of Refuge: A History of Leprosy in Western Australia*, University of Western Australia Press for the Public Health Department, Perth, 1978.

de Waal, Esther, *A Life – Giving Way: A Commentary on the Rule of St Benedict*, Continuum Books, New York, 1995.

Department of Indigenous Affairs, *Reconciling The Past: Government Control of Aboriginal Monies in Western Australia, 1905–1972*, Report of the Stolen Wages Taskforce, Perth, 2008.

Duncan Owen, June, *Mixed Matches: Interracial Marriage in Australia*, University of New South Wales Press, Sydney, 2002.

Durack, Mary, *The Rock and the Sand*, 1st edn, The Anchor Press, London, 1969.

Edmonds, Leigh, *The Vital Link*, UWA Press, Perth, 1997.

Fletcher, Jack, *To Dam or be Damned: The Mighty Fitzroy River*, self published, Perth, 2008.

Fraser, P, 'Phillipena Fraser' in Brigida Nailon and Francis Huegel (eds), *This is Your Place: Beagle Bay Mission, 1890–1990: Birthplace and Cradle of Catholic Presence in the Kimberley*, Beagle Bay Community with assistance from Magabala Books, Broome, 1990.

Freeth, P, *Born to be a Drover: The Life Story of Jim Freeth*, Hesperian Press, Perth, 2004.

Gammage, B, *The Biggest Estate on Earth: How Aborigines Made Australia*, Allen & Unwin, Sydney, 2011.

Godbehear, Harold S, *Kimberley was God's*, Hesperian Press, Perth, 2011.

Goodall, Heather, Ghosh, Devleena, and Todd, Lindi Renier, 'Jumping ship – skirting empire: Indians, Aborigines and Australians across the Indian Ocean', *Transforming Cultures eJournal*, vol. 3, no. 1, 2008, pp. 44–74, http://epress.lib.uts.edu.au/journals/TfC.

Grimwade, Gordon, 'The Canning Stock Route: desert stock route to outback tourism', *Australasian Historical Archaeology*, vol. 16, 1998, pp. 70–79.

Gugeri, Michael, *God before Gugeri: Luggers, Trucks & Water Bores & Other Kimberley Stories*, Hesperian Press, Perth, 2014.

Hattersley, Colleen (ed.), *Birr Nganka Nyikina: The Source of Nyikina Language with reference to Lower Nyikina*, Madjulla Inc, Broome, 2014.

Hawke, Stephen, and Gallagher, Michael, *Noonkanbah: Whose Land, Whose Law*, Fremantle Arts Centre Press, Fremantle, 1989.

Hess, Michael, 'Black and red: the Pilbara pastoral workers' strike, 1946', *Aboriginal History*, vol. 18, no. 1, 1994, pp. 65–83.

Hewitt, David, *A Brief History of the Canning Stock Route*, Canning Stock Route Aerial Tours, East Victoria Park, 1980.

Hoorn, Jeanette, *Australian Pastoral: The Making of White Landscape*, Fremantle Press, Fremantle, 2007.

Hough, David, *Boans for Service: The Story of a Department Store 1895–1986*, The Estate of FT Boan, Claremont, WA, 2009.

'How to pronounce Nyikina', adapted from 'Guide to writing languages of the Kimberley', Kimberley Language Resource Centre, Halls Creek, 2000.

Jarlmadangah Aboriginal Community, *Woonyoomboo: A Story from Jarlmadangah Community*, Pearson, Melbourne, 2010.

Jebb, Mary Ann, *Blood, Sweat and Welfare: A History of White Bosses and Aboriginal Pastoral Workers*, UWA Press, Perth, 2002.

Jordan, Ann, 'From bartering to bills: the history of money', *Appleseeds*, vol. 7, no. 7, 2005.

Kabir, N, 'Muslims in Western Australia 1870–1970', *Early Days: Journal of the Royal Western Australian Historical Society*, vol. 12, no. 5, 2005, pp. 550–565.

Keene, Judith, '"The word makes the man": a Catalan anarchist autodidact in the Australian bush', *Australian Journal of Politics and History*, vol. 47, no. 3, 2001, pp. 311–329.

Kneipp, Mary, 'Australian Catholics and the Spanish Civil War', *Journal of the Australian Catholic Historical Society*, vol. 19, 1998, pp. 47–64.

Lamidey, Noel W, *Aliens Control in Australia*, N Lamidey, Sydney, 1974.

'Liveringa': The Property of the Kimberley Pastoral Company, Limited, Cyclopedia Co, Perth, 1912.

Lockyer, Betty, *Last Truck Out*, Magabala Books, Broome, 2009.

Lynch, Tom, 'Nothing but land: women's narratives, gardens, and the settler-colonial imaginary in the U.S. west and Australian outback', *Western American Literature*, vol. 48, no. 4, 2014, pp. 374–399.

Marshall, Lucy, *Reflections of a Kimberley Woman*, Madjulla Inc, Broome, 2004.

Marshall, Paul (ed.), *Raparapa Kularr Martuwarra: All Right, Now We Go 'Side the River, Along That Sundown Way: Stories from the Fitzroy River Drovers*, Magabala Books, Broome, 1988.

McGrath, Ann, *Born in the Cattle: Aborigines in Cattle Country*, Allen & Unwin, Sydney, 1987.

McGregor, William B, 'Language shift among the Nyulnyul of Dampier land: Acta Linguistica Hafniensia', *International Journal of Linguistics*, vol. 35, no. 1, 2003, pp. 115–159.

McKenzie, Maisie, *The Road to Mowanjum*, Angus & Robertson, Melbourne, 1969.

McLeod, DW, *How the West was Lost: The Native Question in the Development of Western Australia*, self-published, Port Hedland, 1984.

Milgin, Annie Nayina, Watson, John Dadakar, and Thompson, Liz, *Living with the Land: Bush Tucker and Medicine of the Nyikina*, Pearson Library, Sydney, 2009.

Morgan, David L, 'Fish fauna of the Fitzroy River in the Kimberley region of Western Australia: including Bunuba, Gooniyandi, Ngarinyin, Nyikina and Walmajarri Aboriginal names', *Records of the Western Australian Museum*, vol. 22, no. 22, 2004, pp. 141–167.

Mowaljarlai, David, and Mainic, Jutta, *Yorro Yorro: Everything Standing Up Alive*, Magabala Books, Broome, 1993.

Nailon, Brigida, *Encounter: The Past and Future of Remote Kimberley*, Echuca, Vic, Brigidine Sisters, c. 2009.

Neumann, Klaus, 'The stench of the past: revisionism in Pacific Islands and Australian history', *Contemporary Pacific*, vol. 10, no. 1, 1998, pp. 31–64.

Neumann, Klaus, *In the Interest of National Security: Civilian Internment in Australia during World War 2*, National Archives of Australia, Canberra, 2006.

Neville, Auber Octavius, *Australia's Coloured Minority: Its Place in the Community*, Currawong Publishing Co, Sydney, c. 1948.

Niall, Brenda, *True North: The Story of Mary and Elizabeth Durack*, Text Publishing, Melbourne, 2012.

Nixon, Marion, *The Rivers of Home*, Vanguard Service Print, Perth, 1978.

Nugent, Maria, '"Every right to be there": cinema spaces and racial politics in Baz Luhrmann's *Australia*', in Monique Rooney and Russell Smith (eds), *Australian Humanities Review*, no. 51, 2011, pp. 5–23.

O'Brien, Anne, *God's Willing Workers: Women and Religion in Australia*, University of NSW Press, Sydney, 2005.

Owen, Chris, 'The police appear to be a useless lot up there: law and order in the East Kimberley 1884–1905', *Aboriginal History*, vol. 27, 2003, pp. 105–130.

Owen, Chris, *'Every Mother's Son is Guilty...': Policing the Kimberley Frontier of Western Australia 1882–1905*, UWA Publishing, Perth, 2016.

Pascoe, Bruce, *Dark Emu: Aboriginal Australia and the Birth of Agriculture*, Magabala Books, Broome, 2018.

Perez, Eugene, *Kalumburu: The Benedictine Mission and the Aborigines, 1908–1975*, Kalumburu Benedictine Mission, Perth, 1977.

Pratt, Rosemary, and Millington, John (eds), *The Torres Diaries, 1910–1914: Diaries of Dom Fulgentius (Anthony) Torres y Mayans, O.S.B, Abbot Nullius of New Norcia*, 'Kalumburu War Diary', Artlook Books, Perth, 1987.

Purcell, Brad, *Dingo*, CSIRO Publishing, Melbourne, 2010.

Raikowski, Pamela, *Linden Girl: The Story of Outlawed Lives*, UWA Press, Perth, 1995.

Ridley, Joan, *To Wallal and Back: The Story of a Mullewa Drover*, Hesperian Press, Perth, 1999.

Rowse, Tim (ed.), *Contesting Assimilation*, API Network, Curtin University, Perth, c. 2005.

Ryan, Lyndall, and Dwyer, Philip G (eds), *Theatres of Violence: Massacre, Mass Killing, and Atrocity Throughout History*, Berghahn Books, New York, 2012.

Sarantakos, Sotirios, 'Quality of family life on the farm', *Journal of Family Studies*, vol. 6, no. 2, 2000, pp. 182–198.

Scrimgeour, Anne, 'Battlin' for their rights: Aboriginal activism and the leper line', *Aboriginal History*, vol. 36, 2012, pp. 43–65.

Scrimgeour, Anne, 'We only want our rights and freedom: the Pilbara pastoral workers strike, 1946–1949', *History Australia*, vol. 11, no. 2, 2014, pp. 101–124.

Semeniuk, V, and Brocx, M, 'King Sound and the tide-dominated delta of the Fitzroy River: their geoheritage values', *Journal of the Royal Society of Western Australia*, vol. 94, no. 2, 2011, pp. 151–160.

Shilling, D, 'The birds of Upper Liveringa Station, Western Australia', *Emu*, vol. 48, no. 1, 1948, pp. 64–72.

'Slipstream: official publication of MacRobertson Miller Airlines Ltd.', *The Airlines*, vol. 4, no. 10, 1960.

Smith, Tony, 'Aboriginal labour and the pastoral industry in the Kimberley division of Western Australia: 1960–1975', *Journal of Agrarian Change*, vol. 3, no. 4, 2003, pp. 552–570.

Spalding, P, *Self-harvest: A Study of Diaries and the Diarist*, Independent Press, London, 1949.

Stephenson, Peta, *Islam Dreaming: Indigenous Muslims in Australia*, UNSW Press, Sydney, 2010.

Stokes, B, Johnston, G, and Marshall, L, *First Nyikina Dictionary – Draft*, Kimberley Language Resource Centre, Fitzroy Crossing, 2000.

The Story of the Air Beef Project in North West Australia, FH Johnston for Air Beef, Sydney, 1951.

Trengove, Alan, 'Essington Lewis', *What's Good for Australia...! The Story of BHP*, Cassell Australia, Stanmore, NSW, 1975.

Tuan, Yi-Fu, *Space and Place: The Perspective of Experience*, University of Minnesota Press, Minneapolis, 1977.

Turnbull, PL, *A Lifetime Of Caring: The History of the Leprosy Mission in Australia, 1913–1988*, Leprosy Mission, Melbourne, 1990.

Uren, Malcolm, and Parrick, F, *Servant of the State: The History of the Main Roads Department 1926–1976*, Commissioner of Main Roads, Perth, 1976.

Williams, Magdalene, *Ngay janijirr ngank = This Is My Word*, Magabala Books, Broome, 1999.

Wright, Edie, *Full Circle: From Mission to Community: A Family Story*, Fremantle Arts Centre Press, Fremantle, 2001.

Wybourne, Catherine, *Work & Prayer: The Rule of St Benedict for Lay People*, Continuum Books, London, 1992.

Zucker, Margaret, *From Patrons to Partners: A History of the Catholic Church in the Kimberley*, University of Notre Dame Australia Press, Fremantle, 1994.

Audio and film

Blue Streak rocket program heritage listed, dir. Vanessa Mills, Australian Broadcasting Commission, Kimberley, 2013, http://www.abc.net.au/local/audio/2010/11/09/3061650.htm.

Brann, Matt, "*The Kimberley Flock*, ABC Rural, 10 November 2010.

I Grew Up as a Jillaroo, dir. Leena Fraser, Australian Broadcasting Commission, 2014, https://soundcloud.com/abcwa/i-grew-up-as-a-jillaroo-meet-lena-buckle-fraser.

The Joybeats live on in the Kimberley, dir. Hilary Smale, Australian Broadcasting Commission, Kimberley, 2012, http://www.abc.net.au/local/audio/2012/09/26/3598312.htm.

Whispering in Our Hearts: The Mowla Bluff Massacre, dir. Mitch Torres, Australian Films Finance Corporation, Canberra, in association with SBS Independent, Ronin Films, c. 2001.

Yajilarra – to dream: Aboriginal women leading change in remote Australia, dir. M. Hogan, Marninwarntikura Women's Resource Centre, Fitzroy Valley, 2009.

Online sources

Anderson, R, *First Port in the Northwest: A Maritime Archaeological Survey of Cossack 25–30 June 2012*, Western Australian Museum, Perth, 2013, http://museum.wa.gov.au/maritime-archaeology-db/sites/default/files/no._297_cossack_ma_survey_2012.pdf.

Beagle Bay (1890–2000), German Missionaries in Australia, Griffith University, http://missionaries.griffith.edu.au/mission/beagle-bay-1890-2000.

Canning Stock Route, Wikipedia, 29 October 2019, https://en.wikipedia.org/wiki/Canning_Stock_Route.

Koombana Days, Chapter 6, 'The great divide', http://www.koombanadays.com/ch06/idx/kd06il0.html#p97.

Mardoowarra, Madjulla Inc., 11 March 2016, http://majala.com.au/mardoowarra/.

Pascoe, Bruce, *A real history of Aboriginal Australians, the first agriculturalists*, TEDxSydney, 15 June 2018, https://tedxsydney.com/

talk/a-real-history-of-aboriginal-australians-the-first-agricultural-ists-bruce-pascoe/.

Rosalía de Castro: Was she a dangerous woman?, Dangerous Women Project, 8 June 2016, http://dangerouswomenproject.org/2016/06/08/rosalia-de-castro/.

SS Koombana, Wikipedia, 5 April 2020, https://en.wikipedia.org/wiki/SS_Koombana.

'The history of Cossack', *Hamersley News*, 26 April 1979, p. 16, https://trove.nla.gov.au/newspaper/article/214548640.

Wroth, D, *The Canning Stock Route*, Japingka Aboriginal Art, https://japing-kaaboriginalart.com/articles/the-canning-stock-route/.